E. W. KENYON

PERSONAL EVANGELISM

22 LESSONS TO EFFECTIVELY SHARE THE GOSPEL

WHITAKER
HOUSE

PERSONAL EVANGELISM
22 Lessons to Effectively Share the Gospel

Kenyon's Gospel Publishing Society
P.O. Box 973
Lynnwood, WA 98046-0973
www.kenyons.org

ISBN: 978-1-64123-806-9

Printed in the United States of America
© 2022 Kenyon's Gospel Publishing Society

Whitaker House
1030 Hunt Valley Circle
New Kensington, PA 15068
www.whitakerhouse.com

Library of Congress Control Number: 2021949582

1 2 3 4 5 6 7 8 9 10 11 ⨆⨆ 28 27 26 25 24 23 22 21

CONTENTS

1

THE SOUL-WINNING BUSINESS

Until soul winning becomes the business of our life, we will not lead many men from darkness to light.

Soul winning is the art of arts. We should study carefully the lives and methods of the great soul winners. Get every book possible on the subject, but never neglect the Bible by being so occupied with other books.

"He that winneth souls is wise" (Proverbs 11:30). You can see it is the world's greatest business proposition.

Think what it can mean! You are tied up with Jesus Christ in winning individuals to Him. It is a divine drama—taking men out of the hands of the enemy, out of bondage, failure, and weakness, and giving them strength, joy, and success.

Jesus likened it to fishing. He said, *"Follow me, and I will make you fishers of men"* (Matthew 4:19).

A fisherman is a skilled man. We should study to show ourselves approved unto God, soul winners who need not be ashamed in the way we handle the Word.

We are selling the greatest thing in the world. It brings the greatest joy, success, and dividends. The joy that it gives to the one who finds Christ, the blessings that go into the home, can never be estimated.

The man you lead to Christ may become a key man in some community, turning a whole section of men to Christ.

You want to realize that you have been engaged by the Master to do this kind of work, that your time is not your own, and that every unsaved man is an opportunity.

You are selling the greatest blessing, and the price you are asking is their confession of the lordship of Jesus and their acceptance of Him as their Savior.

For every soul you win, you get stars in your crown.

They get eternal life and blessings beyond words.

Here are some suggestions:

+ Never ask a man if he is saved.
+ Never tell him he must repent, or go to hell.
+ Give him the Word and he will repent.
+ Be courteous; be very kind. *"Be ye therefore wise as serpents, and harmless as doves"* (Matthew 10:16).
+ Get alone with your prospect if you can.
+ Never argue. Answer all questions from the Word.
+ Be firm, but gentle.
+ If he asks questions you cannot answer, acknowledge it. Never bluff, never show off.

Remember, you are dealing with eternal personalities. That person is eternal, and you are dealing with eternal issues.

Win their confidence and then win them with the Word. Show them gently and tenderly that because of Adam's sin in the garden, man died spiritually and lost his standing with God.

> *And the* Lord *God commanded the man, saying, Of every tree of the garden thou mayest freely eat: but of the tree of the knowledge of good and evil, thou shalt not eat of it: for in the day that thou eatest thereof thou shalt surely die.*
>
> (Genesis 2:16–17)

Adam died spiritually and was driven from the garden the day that he ate the forbidden fruit. His physical death took place some 930 years later.

"Death passed upon all men" (Romans 5:12).

Since the time of Adam, every man except Christ has been spiritually dead, and the evil that is in the world is an outcropping of the death that is in man's spirit.

Spiritual death shows itself more plainly in some people than in others. Take the case of a criminal; it is easy to see how he could be spiritually dead. But in the case of an honest, good-living man, it is not manifested so openly. Yet, he too is spiritually dead.

God's Word declares it. First Samuel 16:7 explains this: *"For man looketh on the outward appearance, but the* Lord *looketh on the heart."*

We see only a man's conduct and a man may justify himself in the eyes of men by his good manner of life.

God looks on the heart, or the man's spirit, and it is here that spiritual death is lodged. Knowing this, that every man outside of Christ is spiritually dead, we can see that Jesus Christ offers the only solution to man's need.

In John 10:10, He tells us, *"I am come that they might have life."* This is eternal life, the nature and life of God, imparted to man's spirit, making him an actual son of God, a new creature with a new nature.

The following Scriptures show how to receive eternal life:

+ Isaiah 53:6: *"All we like sheep have gone astray; we have turned every one to his own way; and the* LORD *hath laid on him the iniquity of us all."* Our redemption has been purchased, and our penalty paid. It remains for us to accept it.

+ John 1:12 (DBY): *"But as many as received him, to them gave he the right to be children of God, to those that believe on his name."*

+ Romans 10:9–10 tells how one may receive Christ, and thus become a child of God: *"If thou shalt confess with thy mouth the Lord Jesus, and shalt believe in thine heart that God hath raised him from the dead, thou shalt be saved. For with the heart man believeth unto righteousness; and with the mouth confession is made unto salvation."*

It is a heart affair. A man believes in his heart and confesses with his mouth. When he does this, God gives him eternal life. The Word of God that he has acted upon is his evidence of salvation.

Joy may come as a result of what has taken place, but the real evidence of salvation is the Word of God, which says that if he believes in his heart and confesses with his mouth, he is saved.

The closing of the "deal"—getting the man to make the actual decision—is the most important thing, the thing that counts. You are rewarded for the deals closed, not the number of deals started.

Results are the only things that count. Your arguments, your logic, your talking do not mean a thing unless you are able to bring a man to make a decision for Christ.

Go out and win them for the Master.

The most effective aid to personal work is a thorough knowledge of the Bible. This can be obtained by a careful study of our Bible study course, *The Bible in the Light of Our Redemption*.

This book on personal evangelism is not intended to take the place of the Bible study course, but to enable you to use more effectively your knowledge of the Word.

QUESTIONS

1. Explain Matthew 4:19.
2. Why does the unsaved man need eternal life?
3. What does the unsaved man have to do to obtain eternal life?
4. What is the real evidence of salvation?
5. What us the main object of personal work?

2

HOLDING FORTH THE WORD OF LIFE

It is only by acting on God's Word that a man can receive eternal life. Therefore it is absolutely necessary that the unsaved man come into contact with the living Word of God, and be made to realize his need of eternal life and how to receive it.

There is no way quite as effective as for him to hear the Word from the lips of someone who really believes it and has a loving interest in his personal salvation.

> That ye may be blameless and harmless, the sons of God, without rebuke, in the midst of a crooked and perverse nation, among whom ye shine as lights in the world; holding forth the word of life.   (Philippians 2:15–16)

We are to hold forth the *"word of life,"* this vital living message from the heart of God. It is our privilege to offer a message to those who will embrace it. We are not to hold the Word, but we are to hold it forth in an inviting, cheerful manner.

It is not enough for us to have the Word in our own lives and be enjoying the realities of redemption. Jesus Christ would have us be channels through which He can send out a message of life and freedom already purchased and awaiting those in bondage.

A NEW LIFE

If we could only realize that in this day and age, people are interested in something that can cope with their economic and social problems rather than a religion. The world is full of religion.

Religion doesn't offer a solution for the problems of today. If it did, there would be no need for writing this lesson.

We do not have a religion to offer the unsaved. We have eternal life, the nature of God. It will make them new creations, which will solve the problems of their lives.

C. H. Yatman has said that tact was common sense put to work. We believe it to be more than that. Tact is love dominating our lives so that as we approach the unsaved, we will have the very wisdom of Christ, which is born of love.

A TACTFUL APPROACH

The "how" to reach men, how to approach them, is perhaps the most difficult problem that confronts the worker. But the Holy Spirit is bound to show us the way of approach.

I have found that when I became burdened for a soul, God was dealing with that soul at the same time, which made the approach easy.

Romans 5:5 tells us, "*The love of God is shed abroad in our hearts.*" We know we have passed from death unto life because we love.

The personal worker must walk in the fullest fellowship with the Father. The person with whom he is dealing must have a consciousness of His love for him, of His desire to help him.

If a man sees that you love him and are really interested in him, he opens up to you. He makes it easy for you to speak to him.

If your heart has been burdened for a person, you can be sure that he is ready for your message.

Never tell him what he must give up. Take the other side of the issue. Tell him what he will gain, the joy and blessing it will bring to his home and life. All the while you are speaking, keep your heart open toward God so He can guide you as you present Jesus to the man.

A SAMPLE APPROACH

A man addressed an acquaintance of his in a warm, friendly manner with the following words:

"John, I am rather anxious about your salvation. I know it will mean so much to you and your family, and I want you to have the thing that has made such changes in my home. Let me give you one or two Scriptures that will help you."

He immediately had his friend's attention and was able to sow the seed that eventually led his friend into the family of God.

WIN THEM BY THE WORD

God's Message is a living and active power, sharper than any two-edged sword, piercing its way till it penetrates soul and spirit.   (Hebrews 4:12 TCNT)

The Word of God alone can bring conviction and penetrate the spiritual darkness that the unsaved man is striving in.

It is not our words. It is God's Word that grips the heart and convinces a man of his need of Christ.

You cannot always lead a man to Christ the first time you talk to him. Most likely, you will find it necessary to speak to him several times.

Now the secret of making your work effective is this: each time you contact your prospect, leave with him a Scripture to think about.

Human words and reasoning get no further than a man's intellect, but the Word of God reaches down into his very heart and really gets hold of him.

The Word alone has the power of awakening a man from his spiritual stupor and causing him to turn resolutely to the Lord.

I have found this to be true, that one or two Scriptures read and explained to the man you are dealing with has much more effect than hours of reasoning and talking religion.

It is the living Word that brings life.

QUESTIONS

1. What do we mean by *"holding forth the word of life"*?
2. Describe the difference between religion and eternal life.
3. How can you approach an unsaved man without offending him?
4. Why is it necessary to use the Word of God?

3

SPEAKING THE TRUTH IN LOVE

As "fishers of men" employed by Jesus Christ, we must do our work in a spirit that will reflect Christ's attitude toward the world.

Christ is the head of a mighty organization engaged in taking men out of the dominion of Satan and bringing them into the realm of love and life eternal. The love of Christ must dominate the actions of every person who takes part in this great work, from the foremost Christian leader to the quietly working but unnoticed layman.

> Foolish and unlearned questions avoid, knowing that they do gender strifes. And the servant of the Lord must not strive; but be gentle unto all men, apt to teach, patient, in meekness instructing those that oppose themselves.
>
> (2 Timothy 2:23–25)

We must under no circumstances be drawn into an argument, as nothing can be gained by it. You will find that it is very difficult to win an argument and a soul at the same time.

It is so very important that we remember this, as so many precious eternal beings are driven away by some unwise person who could not control his tongue.

Some unsaved men will try to draw you into a sharp discussion so that they can show off their knowledge of science or evolution, or some other subject.

Avoid such useless discussions, as your purpose is not to reason with men concerning personal opinions but to convey to them a message from God's Word.

You are a messenger and it is not your place to argue with men about the message, but it is your duty to deliver it to them.

A soft answer turneth away wrath: but grievous words stir up anger. (Proverbs 15:1)

It never pays to be overcome by any situation, no matter how difficult. If the person with whom you are conversing seems rather harsh, discourteous, or ill-mannered, then no better method of answer could possibly work than that of remaining master of the situation by your gentle, loving spirit.

Always strive to speak the right word at the right time. The conversation should positively suit the situation. Be calm in your tone of speech, *never* become excited, worked up, or argumentative.

In a meeting being conducted by a young Christian worker, there was a high school student present who was unsaved and full of skepticism. The meeting was of such a nature that it was not out of place to ask questions, which he did.

His very irritating and annoying manner could have easily given rise to an argument. In spite of the situation, the young worker kept calm, answering his questions to the best of his ability, but refusing to argue.

There happened to be other unsaved people present who were impressed by this. Had a heated discussion taken place, it would have greatly lessened his chances of leading them to Christ.

Later in the evening, the student himself accepted Christ.

For the wrath of man worketh not the righteousness of God. (James 1:20)

USE OF TRACTS

Many times, it is impossible to speak personally to an individual whom we contact. In crowded places such as street cars, trains, buses, or large gatherings, it is often well to quietly hand a tract to those whom we meet. Everyone can give out tracts. Everyone should possess a good supply of tracts that clearly and simply explain the need and way of salvation.

Over every tract, the personal worker should breathe a prayer in the name of Jesus. He says, *"Whatsoever ye shall ask the Father in my name, he will give it you"* (John 16:23).

How limitless the ministry of tracts can become.

Always carry a good selection of tracts. Always be looking for opportunities to give them away. Thousands have been saved because someone was faithful in handing out tracts.

After you have led a man to Christ, it would be well to give him several tracts to give out, so that he can start right in working for the Lord.

THE PERSONAL WORKER MUST BE A LOVER OF SOULS

The greatest qualification for a successful personal worker is a genuine love for men and women. The successful personal worker's attitude is this: "I love as though I had died for them."

If a Christian discovers that he does not possess this love, he may receive it by claiming it in Christ. *"My God shall supply all your need"* (Philippians 4:19).

He will meet this need of love.

Meditation in the Word will also bring to us love for the unsaved and show to us our responsibilities as personal workers.

All things are of God, who hath reconciled us to himself by Jesus Christ, and hath given to us the ministry of reconciliation; to

*wit, that God was in Christ, reconciling the world unto him-
self, not imputing their trespasses unto them; and hath committed unto us the word of reconciliation. Now then we are
ambassadors for Christ.*   (2 Corinthians 5:18–20)

God has completely reconciled the world unto Himself, but
we must bring to them the message of reconciliation. The ministry
of reconciliation in Christ will be of no effect if we do not bring it
to them.

If a man could be saved without hearing the gospel, Christ
would not have given the Great Commission:

*Go therefore and make disciples of all the nations; baptize
them into the name of the Father, and of the Son, and of the
Holy Spirit.*   (Matthew 28:19 wey)

We are His ambassadors. God is beseeching through us. He
has no other contact with the lost world. This is why we must love
them as Christ loved them. We must be as anxious to bring to
them the message of reconciliation as though we had, in the place
of Christ, died for their redemption.

You must have a fixed goal before you in dealing with an
unsaved person whom you are endeavoring to lead to Christ. Your
purpose in bringing the Word to him is to receive from him a confession of the lordship of Jesus Christ over his life.

QUESTIONS

1. What one characteristic is to be outstanding in the per-
    sonal worker?

2. Why is it best never to argue with the unsaved?

3. Why should one carry tracts or other Christian litera-
    ture with them at all times?

4. Can a man be born again without ever hearing the Word
    of God?

4

THE APPROACH

Jesus gave us an example of speaking to others about things that interested them. When He was with farmers, He spoke in parables about the soil. (See Matthew 13:3–8, 24–32.)

We should likewise adapt our speech to the people with whom we are dealing. Talk about subjects in which they are interested. Get them to express themselves; do not do all of the talking. By your tone of voice and words, show a real interest in them.

The art of knowing *where*, *how*, *when*, and *what* to converse is the height of personal work efficiency. We may possess a knowledge of the Word of God, but if we lack wisdom, our efforts will be of no influence or real benefit.

By the grace of God, we should strive to attain to the highest possible quality of speech that will build for eternity. (See 1 Corinthians 3:10.)

BE TACTFUL IN YOUR APPROACH

It is very important to have tact in your approach, but in your desire to use tact, do not neglect the introduction of the subject of salvation.

Be prayerful in your approach. Pray silently before you speak.

Be sympathetic. Never have a "holier than thou" attitude. Even with those who have gone into deep sin, as we call it, we can truly say and feel, "Did not God have great love to send His Son into the world to die for sinners like you and me?"

Be patient but persistent. You are dealing with a soul whose destiny is at stake.

> *These are they who in an honest and good heart, having heard the word keep it, and bring forth fruit with patience.*
>
> (Luke 8:15 DBY)

Do not be discouraged. It is Satan's greatest tool in personal work.

Know that you are sowing the seed, the Word of God. It will bring forth fruit. Remember, God has said, "*So shall my word be that goeth forth out of my mouth: it shall not return unto me void, but it shall accomplish that which I please, and it shall prosper in the thing whereto I sent it*" (Isaiah 55:11).

When Satan even whispers, "It's no use to speak to that person; it won't do any good," remember Isaiah 33:6: "*Wisdom and knowledge shall be the stability of thy times, and strength of salvation: the fear of the LORD is his treasure.*"

DECISION TIME

There is a time of sowing, but remember, the decision you bring forth is the reaping time. If you do not give one the chance to decide, you are often missing a chance to win a soul.

> *If thou shalt confess with thy mouth the Lord Jesus, and shalt believe in thine heart that God hath raised him from the dead, thou shalt be saved. For with the heart man believeth unto*

righteousness; and with the mouth confession is made unto salvation.   (Romans 10:9–10)

You will find these Scriptures to be invaluable. When they become a living reality in your life, you can use them with confidence and assurance.

We have the one who wants to make the decision act on Romans 10:9. Before you have them repeat this verse, you must explain each part.

Give them Acts 2:36 and Hebrews 2:14. Show them that man's need can only be met by the lordship of Christ over his life.

Give them Colossians 1:13 (DBY): *"Who has delivered us from the authority of darkness, and translated us into the kingdom of the Son of his love."*

You see, the only way to salvation is to confess this new lordship of Christ. Hitherto everyone has been under the lordship of Satan. Have them confess in words, "I take Christ as my Savior and Lord."

Then you show them that righteousness has been purchased by Christ for all.

He hath made him to be sin for us, who knew no sin; that we might be made the righteousness of God in him.
                                    (2 Corinthians 5:21)

When a man confesses this lordship, he receives this nature of God, His righteousness. You have him say, "I believe that God has raised Christ from the dead." When Christ arose, everyone was justified. Then by all means, have him clinch the matter by saying, "I know God saves me now."

Many who have been seeking salvation for years have never made this last statement, and they are still only hoping they are saved.

How sad it is to see the lack of understanding there is of the new birth. One can only have the new birth by confession of Christ as their Savior. It is necessary to believe they are saved the moment they do this.

I can hear someone say, "But you make it too easy."

Well, what works can a spiritually dead man do to make the redemptive work of Christ more complete? No, it is not what we do in the line of penance or repentance that will give us the power to become children of God. (See John 1:12.)

THE KIND OF CHRISTIAN

It is quite a significant fact that whatever you tell of what you are enjoying in Christ, the one you lead to Christ will try to receive. In other words, the men and women you lead to Christ will be the kind of a Christian you are.

That is why God has placed in missions those who have been delivered from bad habits, so they can lead men to accept this freedom from Satan's bondage, or be delivered from drug habit, drinking habit, or another addiction.

I know a woman who had made Christ her burden bearer. One day, she had the opportunity to lead a man to Christ who had many burdens in his home to bear. A week later, she saw the man and his face was just glowing. He said, "I just haven't had a care since I took Christ as my Savior. I have been as a little child, free from all worry."

RIGHTLY DIVIDING

Study to shew thyself approved unto God...rightly dividing the word of truth.   (2 Timothy 2:15)

Some Scriptures are written to spiritually dead men, and some to children of God.

Take for instance, *"There is none righteous, no, not one"* (Romans 3:10). This is not written for Christians, yet it is often applied to them, keeping men and women from taking their places without condemnation before God. (See Romans 8:1.) They then feel too unworthy to bear fruit. The greatest fruit you can bear is prayer. No one comes to God under condemnation and believes he has his petition. God can only work on the law of faith.

Here is another Scripture that is often misused:

> *If we confess our sins, he is faithful and just to forgive us our sins, and to cleanse us from all unrighteousness.* (1 John 1:9)

This is written to Christians, not to the unsaved. Yet, many tracts quote it, saying you must confess every sin you have committed before you can be saved. Those sins were laid on Christ; they have been remitted, blotted out. You could not remember all your sins anyway, but if you could, it would not change the case. Nothing you can do before you accept Christ will change the fact that all your iniquities were laid upon Him. (See Isaiah 53:6.)

But to the Christian, we are admonished to search our hearts daily to see if we have sinned and to confess our sins so we may be cleansed daily from all unrighteousness.

This is a wonderful Scripture to give to the babes in Christ. They will make many mistakes while their minds are being renewed by the Word, and they need to know there is a provision made to keep them in fellowship.

QUESTIONS

1. What can we learn from studying the way Jesus approached people?

2. Give three necessary characteristics in winning souls to Christ.

3. Explain Romans 10:9 as you would explain it to the unsaved.

4. What in your life will influence the new convert?

5. Give two Scriptures that are often given to the wrong class. Explain.

5

THE PERSONAL WORKER'S ABILITY

You will receive power when the Holy Spirit has come upon you, and you will be my witnesses in Jerusalem and in all Judaea and Samaria and to the remotest parts of the earth.

(Acts 1:8 WEY)

This is a challenge to every personal worker. Before Christ left this earth, leaving His followers to carry on His message of redemption, He told them that they would receive the ability to be His witnesses after the Holy Spirit came.

The only thing that will make us effectual workers for the Master is our using this ability. In order to help us understand this ability, we are going to study it from two angles.

First, the Holy Spirit gives us the ability to keep the one command that Christ gave to us in John 13:34: *"Love one another."*

Without this love that loves as Christ loves, no one can ever become a real soul winner. The love that compelled the Son of God to give His life for lost man is the only motivating force that will compel us to give our lives to win that man for Christ.

25

As we stand before this commandment in our own strength, we are absolutely helpless. How can we human beings love as the Son of God loves? How can we generate that divine love that will cause us to be known by the world as His disciples?

The only answer to these questions is found in Acts 1:8. When the Holy Spirit indwells us, He will give us the ability to love as He loves.

"*God is love*" (1 John 4:8). Therefore, the Holy Spirit is love. When the Holy Spirit indwells us, He sheds abroad in our very being the love of God. (See Romans 5:5.)

COMPARISON OF HUMAN AND DIVINE ABILITY

Let us now compare this divine ability that is ours with human ability.

Human ability is inherited, but it must be developed. It is common knowledge that a person of great natural ability will be a failure in life unless he develops the ability that he has.

Many with mediocre ability surpass those of great ability because they consistently work to develop the ability that is theirs.

So it is with this divine ability. It is ours by inheritance, but it must be developed. Every child of God has a right to ask for the indwelling of the Holy Spirit. (See Luke 11:13.)

This divine ability to love must be developed by constant use and practice. It is developed by faith, by acting on Romans 5:5.

One can practice love by doing the thing that he would do if he did love. If you had love for the unsaved man, you would pray for him, and you would speak to him about Christ. Begin to do it.

Begin to practice love toward the unsaved man and you will find that by giving the love of God that is within your expression, it will grow and develop.

Unless you practice love, you will smother it; you will hinder the development of that ability to love.

The Holy Spirit gives us the ability to know the truth. (See John 16:13–15.)

The Holy Spirit gives us the ability to become efficient ambassadors for the Master. We are the only ambassadors for Christ. (See 2 Corinthians 5:19–20.)

We are the only ones who have the message of reconciliation for the world. Angels desire to look into the truths that the Holy Spirit has revealed to us. (See 1 Peter 1:12.)

Would God give to us this important mission without equipping us for it?

He has sent us the Holy Spirit to give us the ability to use the Word of God to lead men and women to Christ.

We must, however, study the Word of God if we are to know it well enough for the Holy Spirit to use it through us.

This fact should cause us to earnestly study the Word. The great tragedy of the church today is that the majority of Christians, who are the only ambassadors for Christ, do not know the plan of salvation well enough to explain it to an unsaved man.

Unless you know the Word of God, the Holy Spirit is going to be crippled in His ministry through you, for the Word of God is His sword. (See Ephesians 6:17.)

"The Spirit of truth" (John 14:17) is in you. The ability to know the truth is yours, but it must be developed. You must set aside time daily for systematic study of the Word of God in order to develop this ability, just as you would set aside time for daily practice if you were going to develop musical ability.

This book was written for that very purpose, to enable you to develop the abilities that are in you, to know the plan of salvation.

This ability to know the Word of God must also be developed by faith.

There are so many who say, "I do not read the Word because I cannot understand it." You *can* understand it because the Holy Spirit is in you to guide you into the truth. Whenever you study the Word of God, study it by faith, depending upon the Holy Spirit to be your teacher, to guide you.

When you have equipped yourself with the Word of God, depend upon the Holy Spirit to anoint that Word and use it as His sword through your lips.

You can never become an effectual personal worker unless you develop this ability to know the truth.

In the distribution of human ability, there is no law of equality. Men are not created equal in regard to natural abilities. There are some who have great musical ability, while others have none. Some have artistic ability; others do not. Then there are those who are very versatile, having many talents, while others have hardly any.

However, there is no law of inequality in regard to the ability that is imparted by the Holy Spirit.

God has no favorite children. No one is born into His family with special endowments of the Holy Spirit's ability. In the spiritual creation in Christ, all men are created equal.

No child has any more right to ask for the indwelling of the Holy Spirit than you have. Just as a human father will not withhold good gifts from his children, God will not withhold the Spirit from any child of His.

No child of God can have any more ability to love or know the truth than you can.

There are some who have more love, there are some who know the Word better than others, but it is not due to the fact that they have any more ability by inheritance.

The fact that one excels another in music does not mean that he has more innate ability. It may only mean that he has worked harder.

It is due to the fact that they have intelligently developed the ability of God that is within them.

You can excel in love, you can excel in the knowledge of the truth, regardless of natural ability, by developing by faith the ability of the Holy Spirit that is yours.

You can excel as a soul winner, if you drive yourself.

Good fishers are hard workers.

QUESTIONS

1. How does love come into our hearts?
2. What are the essentials for soul winning?
3. Can all have the indwelling Holy Spirit?
4. Can all have God's ability?
5. What is your part in soul winning?

6

APPROACHING THE UNSAVED

QUALIFICATIONS OF THE SUCCESSFUL PERSONAL WORKER

HE MUST BE A POSSESSOR

He must not only be a professor, but also a possessor. He himself must radiate the joy, the deep peace, and sense of security that comes from a life in fellowship with God before he can interest others in accepting Christ as Savior and Lord.

It is not difficult for the one with whom he is dealing to soon detect whether or not he is sincere and earnest concerning the tremendous truth he declares.

Sincerity, however, does not mean a long, sad countenance such as the professional Pharisee possessed.

This Scripture translation is clear concerning this:

But, whenever you fast [or perform a duty], pour perfume on your hair and wash your face, that it may not be apparent to men that you are fasting, but to your Father who is in secret;

> *and your Father—He who sees in secret—will recompense*
> *you.*   (Matthew 6:17–18 wey)

The world is looking for a bright and cheerful countenance. No one enjoys meeting a grouch. The child of God can be cheerful always because his trust in his Father makes him absolutely unafraid in every circumstance.

HE MUST BE A LOVER OF SOULS

The greatest qualification for the successful personal worker is a genuine love for men and women. The successful personal worker's attitude is this: "I love them as though I had died for them."

If a Christian discovers that he does not possess this love, he may receive it by claiming it in Christ. *"My God shall abundantly supply all your need"* (Philippians 4:19 dby). He will meet this need of love.

Meditation in the Word will also bring to us a love for the unsaved and show us our responsibilities as personal workers.

> *All this is the work of God, who reconciled us to himself*
> *through Christ, and gave us the Ministry of Reconciliation—*
> *to proclaim that God, in Christ, was reconciling the world to*
> *himself, not reckoning men's offenses against them, and that he*
> *had entrusted us with the Message of this reconciliation. It is,*
> *then, on Christ's behalf that we are acting as ambassadors.*
>   (2 Corinthians 5:18–20 tcnt)

God has completely reconciled the world unto Himself, but we must bring to them the message of reconciliation. The ministry of reconciliation in Christ will be of no effect if we do not bring it to them.

If a man could be saved without hearing the gospel, Christ would not have given the commission: *"Go therefore and make disciples of all the nations; baptize them into the name of the Father, and of the Son, and of the Holy Spirit"* (Matthew 28:19 WEY).

We are His ambassadors. God is beseeching through us. He has no other contact with the lost world. This is why we must love them as Christ loved them. We must be as anxious to bring to them the message of reconciliation as though we had, in the place of Christ, died for their redemption.

It was this love that made David Livingstone a successful missionary in the heart of Africa. Many whom he had contacted had not been able to understand the language he had spoken, but long after he passed from them, whenever his name was mentioned, their faces shone with joy. They had not been able to understand his words, but they had understood the love that burned in his own heart for them. All with whom we contact will respond to the love of Christ within our hearts for them.

HE MUST BE A WISE FISHERMAN

Wisdom belongs to us as our inheritance in Christ.

"But of him are ye in Christ Jesus, who of God is made unto us wisdom" (1 Corinthians 1:30). In every situation, Christ knew just what to say and what to do. His wisdom is ours. For every difficult situation that we encounter, we may claim His wisdom, His understanding of the situation.

In every instance, we must be courteous and considerate of the person with whom we are dealing. A personal worker must never lose his temper, become impatient or argumentative. We are more anxious to win souls than to win an argument.

With His wisdom, what can hinder anyone from becoming a most successful soul winner?

HE MUST BE ALERT IN THE KING'S BUSINESS AND ACTIVE IN HIS SERVICE

The first step in becoming a personal worker is starting, right now, to work toward the saving of precious souls.

Regardless of how awkward or feeble one may feel that his efforts are, it is certainly better to begin today than to wait until he becomes more scientific in his methods. Waiting to become an efficient personal worker has the same results as waiting to be saved.

A person who says, "I cannot do personal work because I do not know how to do it" may be compared to someone who says, "I cannot go into the water until I learn to swim."

Efficiency is the result of experience. Experience is the best practical teacher. Although one is not experienced when he first begins, people will respect and respond to one who brings them a positive, simple, earnest entreaty concerning Christ as Savior.

Many inexperienced young workers have been honored by God. Regardless of experience, our aim should be to win souls for Christ at every opportunity.

When asked the nature of his business, a certain Christian man replied, "I have a shoe store by which I support myself, but my business is to win souls for Christ."

Many times, it is impossible to speak personally to an individual whom we contact. In crowded places such as street cars, trains, buses, or large gatherings, it is often well to quietly hand a tract to those whom we meet. Everyone can give out tracts. Everyone should possess a good supply of tracts that clearly and simply explain the need and way of salvation.

Over every tract, the personal worker should breathe a prayer in the name of Jesus. He says, "*Whatsoever ye shall ask the Father in my name, he will give it you*" (John 16:23).

How limitless the ministry of tracts can become.

Always carry a good selection of tracts. Always be looking for opportunities to give them away. Thousands have been saved because someone was faithful in handing out tracts.

Everyone may become a successful personal worker. We have all received the same righteousness, the same ability, the same wisdom, and the same love. We all possess the same rights in prayer. If a man will give himself to study, meditation, and prayer, and be on the alert for opportunities, the Lord will prosper his endeavors to win souls.

QUESTIONS

1. Show why the personal worker must be a possessor.

2. Give the greatest qualification for a personal worker.

3. If a Christian feels a lack of wisdom, what should he do?

4. Why should one not wait to become efficient before beginning to do personal work?

5. Why may everyone become a successful personal worker?

7

DEALING WITH THE UNSAVED

HINTS AND SUGGESTIONS

We have studied general conditions for success that concern the worker himself. Now we are going to study some hints and suggestions that will prove very useful and helpful to successful personal work.

SUGGESTIONS CONCERNING THE APPROACH TO AN UNSAVED PERSON

One thing that every personal worker should understand is that he should never approach someone who is being led to Christ by another. It may seem to you that the other personal worker is not presenting Christ in the most successful manner, but do not interrupt. Your interruption may detract and confuse the one who is being led to the point of decision in accepting Christ by an unskilled worker. You should also not stand by, listening to the conversation. The presence of a third party may embarrass the unsaved person so that he will not open his heart freely.

If the other personal worker has failed, you pray that God will give you an opportunity to speak with him later.

On the other hand, do not let another person interrupt you when you are dealing with an unsaved person. If it is at all possible, speak a plain but kind word to prevent the interruption.

Another factor in approaching the unsaved is dependence upon the Holy Spirit for guidance. Seek His guidance to direct you to hearts that are hungry for Christ. In this, there is a general rule to be followed, although there are exceptions. It is usually considered wisest for a person to deal with another who is of the same sex and age. This is not true in every case. If the Holy Spirit leads you differently, follow His guidance. Christian teachers who have had a great deal of experience in this field have found that men usually are more successful in dealing with men, and women with women.

If it is at all possible, get the person with whom you are dealing alone. This taking Christ as Savior and confessing Him as Lord is one of the most personal and sacred of all subjects. No one likes to open his heart in the presence of others on a subject that is very personal and sacred.

Many, from pride and embarrassment, will defend themselves and take a false stand when there are a number present. It is better for one worker to deal with an unsaved person than for several workers. It is also better for one worker to deal with a single person at a time than to deal with a number of them.

If you have several to deal with, work with them one at a time. Many times, a person who could not be led to Christ in the presence of other seekers will open his heart freely when he is alone, and will be brought to a definite, positive decision for Christ.

SUGGESTIONS CONCERNING YOUR ACTUAL DEALING WITH THE UNSAVED PERSON

In this, let your reliance be wholly upon the Holy Spirit and the Word of God. The Holy Spirit has come into the world for this purpose—to convict men and women of unbelief in Christ. (See John 16:8.) Trust Him to give you the words to say to each individual.

The instrument that the Holy Spirit uses is the Word of God. It is His sword. (See Ephesians 6:17.) Therefore, we must be equipped with a working knowledge of the Bible, or we will hinder the working of the Holy Spirit. This does not mean that you must wait until you have mastered the Bible. You study until you possess one or two Scriptures that you can use. Let these Scriptures take hold of your heart. It is better to use one Scripture that has mastered you than several Scriptures that you have not mastered. It is usually well to use just one.

Do not only quote or read the Scripture yourself, but ask the person with whom you are dealing to read it aloud. Here is a good Scripture to use:

> *If thou shalt confess with thy mouth the Lord Jesus, and shalt believe in thine heart that God hath raised him from the dead, thou shalt be saved. For with the heart man believeth unto righteousness; and with the mouth confession is made unto salvation.*   (Romans 10:9–10)

Build this Scripture into the heart of the unsaved person. Show him that if he will believe in his heart that God raised Christ from the dead, and confess with his mouth that he will take Him as Savior and Lord, he has become God's child.

Show him that his salvation is not dependent upon his feelings, but on what God says about it. When he has met these conditions, God declares that he is saved, and no one can question or doubt it.

Make accepting Christ as simple as possible. Show him that when he takes Christ as Savior, God absolutely takes him as His child. Have him confess with his mouth that Jesus is Lord.

In your conversation with an unsaved person, always hold him to the main point of accepting Christ. At times, he will wish to discuss the different denominations, different theories concerning creation, or questions that are irrelevant to the point of accepting Christ. Show him that the real issue is his accepting Christ as Savior and Lord. Show him that these questions may be studied and answered satisfactorily after he has become God's child. Do not be afraid to say, "I do not know" when you are asked a hard, irrelevant, or difficult question. Do not ever become involved in one of these discussions that would cause you to lose your leading him to a definite decision with Christ.

In bringing a person to a definite decision for Christ, do not be in a hurry. Many times, when we are too anxious for immediate results, our work is only superficial. One man with whom slow but thorough work has been done, who has taken Christ as Savior and confessed Him publicly as Lord, is better than a dozen with whom hasty work has been done and who have not actually been born again. It is often well to plant within a man's heart his need and privilege of becoming God's child and leaving this truth to bear fruit in his life. Always leave a man with a Scripture, and after you have left him, pray that the Word will work in his life.

If you have failed in any certain place, after you have left the individual, study it out thoroughly to see why you have failed. If you were at a loss to meet his need with a Scripture, study that portion of Scripture until you can handle it successfully. Then, go back and try again. Success in personal work comes out of many apparent defeats.

Always be very courteous and gentle in your speech with an unsaved person. The subject that you are handling is a very delicate one. You are pointing out to the unsaved person the fact that he is a child of Satan. You must be perfectly frank in revealing his condition from the Word of God, yet at the same time, you must be very courteous and winning in your manner.

Show him that it is not his fault that he is spiritually dead and a child of Satan. Show him that he could not help it, that it came through his identification with Adam. Then show him how adequately God has provided a perfect redemption from that condition. Very kindly show him that although it is not his fault that he is in this condition, it does become his fault if he remains in it after he has been shown the way whereby he can become a child of God. Many Christians who have been well-meaning and sincere have repelled those whom they could have won to Christ because they were not careful in presenting these truths to the individual.

QUESTIONS

1. Why should you never interrupt a person who is endeavoring to lead another to Christ?

2. Upon what should you rely in dealing with an unsaved person?

3. Why is it wrong to be hasty in your dealing with an unsaved person?

4. Give five suggestions for personal work.

5. In the case of failure, what should you do?

8

DEALING WITH SPECIAL CLASSES OF MEN

In the last chapter, we studied different methods that we may use in doing personal work. Here, we will look at specific cases.

We are to meet each individual problem and difficulty with the Word.

Remember that the less you give of your own knowledge and experience, the better it will be. Bring them face to face with Christ in the Word.

There are three general classes of people who are unsaved. You will find many outside these classifications.

First is the indifferent, the people who apparently have not thought about their own personal salvation.

Second is the one who has thought about his salvation and has faced it, but is delaying making the decision.

Third is the one who honestly desires to be saved, but does not seem to know how, or lacks the ability to make the decision.

Don't plan to approach everyone in the same way. You are selling Jesus. You are to be wiser than the adversary who is seeking to hinder that sale.

THE INDIFFERENT CLASS

If they have not been instructed in the Word, it will be necessary to show them that they need a new nature, that they must be recreated.

Read John 3:3–8 to them. Be sure to show them, *"That which is born of the flesh is flesh; and that which is born of the Spirit is spirit"* (verse 6). Make it clear that they must be recreated by God Himself.

They may ask you why they need to be recreated. Give them John 8:44–45 and 1 John 3:10.

Show them that there are two families in the world: the family of God and the family of Satan. Show them that it is not a question of their own good deeds, or of their church attendance, but it is a question of their receiving eternal life, the nature of God.

They are not lost because of some special sin that they have committed, but because they have the wrong nature.

Make it clear that the thing they need is eternal life.

It might be well to call their attention to the fact that there are two kinds of life: natural, human life; and the life that Jesus brought. (See John 10:10; John 5:24; and 1 John 5:13.)

Also tell them that there are two kinds of death: spiritual death and physical death.

Spiritual death is the nature of the adversary. Eternal life is the nature of God the Father.

Make it clear to them that they must receive eternal life.

You notice in John 5:24 that we pass out of death into life, and in Romans 5:12 that death entered the human spirit through sin.

That death is spiritual. There is only one solution to their problem. They must act on John 1:2, John 3:16, John 6:27, and, in conclusion, Romans 10:9–10.

These Scriptures will make the subject clear. The thing this man must do is to accept Christ as Savior and confess Him as his Lord, knowing that God raised Him from the dead, and that the moment he accepts Christ, he becomes the righteousness of God in Christ.

THE ONE WHO IS HALTING BETWEEN TWO OPINIONS

All we like sheep have gone astray; we have turned every one to his own way; and the LORD hath laid on him the iniquity of us all. (Isaiah 53:6)

For God so loved the world, that he gave his only begotten Son, that whosoever believeth in him should not perish, but have everlasting life. (John 3:16)

Jesus is a gift that we must receive thankfully.

For by grace are ye saved through faith; and that not of yourselves: it is the gift of God. (Ephesians 2:8)

Do not use too many Scriptures. Find out the difficulty, the reason that they have not made the decision. It may be that they are bound by a demon of fear. You know that Jesus said, *"In my name they shall cast out demons"* (Mark 16:17 DBY).

I have found that when one is unable to make the decision, if I lay my hands on them gently and say, "In Jesus's name, make the decision; in Jesus's name, the spirit that has held this life in bondage, leave now," they will instantly make the decision for Christ.

I have known but a few who failed to respond when I commanded that power that held them to be broken.

You understand clearly that you are dealing with spiritual forces, which are as real as material forces.

God is a spirit. Satan and demons are spirits. Man is a spirit. Be sure that the moment he has made his confession that he knows he is saved, not because of feeling or emotion, but because he has acted intelligently upon the Word of God. Make him understand that believing is acting on the Word.

You might say this to him, "You know that Jesus died for your sins, don't you? You know that He was raised when He had put your sin away, and that He was raised because He had met every demand of justice, and that on the ground of what He had done, you were justified?" (Romans 4:25 tells us this.)

> He [the Father] *hath made him* [Jesus] *to be sin for us, who knew no sin; that we might be made the righteousness of God in him.* (2 Corinthians 5:21)

He has accepted Christ. He has confessed Him as his Lord. He believes that Christ died for his sins and was raised for his justification. Now he knows by his acceptance of Christ and his confession that he is now a new creation in Christ, and he stands before the Father without condemnation.

THE MAN WHO WANTS TO BECOME A CHRISTIAN BUT DOESN'T KNOW HOW

We have practically covered the ground. First, make it clear that eternal life is the thing that he needs, and that it is a gift from God.

> For by grace are ye saved through faith; and that not of your- selves: it is the gift of God: not of works, lest any man should boast. For we are his workmanship, created in Christ Jesus unto good works, which God hath before ordained that we should walk in them. (Ephesians 2:8–10)

Make him see clearly that salvation is not a result of his giving up sin, being sorry for his sin, or promising not to commit any more sin, but he is saved because he accepts Jesus Christ as his Savior. All of the purposes, plans, confessions, and repenting done by a sinner have no virtue in them whatsoever unless he accepts Jesus Christ as Savior.

Repentance and confession of sin have no value unless one acts upon the Word and takes Christ as is Savior.

God gave Jesus to the world as Savior. He has not taken the gift back. Jesus still belongs to the sinner.

He is God's gift to the lost soul. All that lost soul needs to do is to acknowledge the gift, thank the Giver, and salvation is his.

QUESTIONS

1. Why can't we approach all people in the same way?

2. Name the three general classes of people with whom you may come in contact in doing personal work?

3. Explain the two kinds of life and the two kinds of death.

4. What can you do to aid those who seem to find it hard to come to a decision?

5. Name five points we should make clear to everyone we lead to Christ.

9

DEALING WITH THE INDIFFERENT

In our last lesson, we began to study how to deal with those who are indifferent and careless toward the gospel. This is one of the classes of men that we meet with most frequently. We have studied how to show this group their need of Christ as Savior. Another way to arouse a man from his indifference is to show him what Christ has done for him.

SHOW HIM HIS LEGAL RIGHTS

Most of our preaching to the unsaved has been an effort to bring them under condemnation. As you deal with an unsaved person, show him that he possesses legal rights that he has not used. The legal rights that every man possesses are the following:

- A legal right to righteousness, the ability to stand in the presence of God as free from sin and condemnation as though there had never been sin in the world.
- A legal right to receive the life of God.
- A legal right to walk with God as His son.
- A legal right to healing for his physical body.

✦ A legal right to a life of peace and freedom from anxiety and need.

✦ A legal right to immortality for his physical body, and a home in the new heaven and earth where he shall reign with Christ.

The personal worker must understand these vital truths before he can clearly present them to another. Study and meditate upon our redemption in Christ until you are touched and stirred by the bondage of an unsaved man to spiritual death when he possesses legal, God-given rights to freedom.

Study 2 Corinthians 5:14–21 until it becomes a part of you.

HOW TO SHOW A MAN HIS LEGAL RIGHTS

MAN'S LEGAL RIGHT TO RIGHTEOUSNESS

In the previous lesson, we saw how to show a man his need of a Savior by making clear to him his identification with Adam. In showing a man his legal right to righteousness, show him his identification with Christ, which destroys the effect of his identification with Adam. You will find man's identification with Christ also in Romans 5:12–21.

Show the one with whom you are dealing his legal identification with Christ upon the cross. Explain clearly to him that, in the mind of God, it was man who hung there, not Christ.

Use the following Scriptures: 2 Corinthians 5:21 (God actually made Jesus sin for us); and Galatians 2:20 (man was crucified with Christ).

You will find Isaiah 53:5–6 very effective. It is helpful to have the person you are trying to reach to read these verses aloud, changing the plural pronoun to the singular: *"He was wounded for* [my] *transgressions, he was bruised for* [my] *iniquities."*

Center your explanation of man's legal right to righteousness on Romans 4:25 (YLT): "*Who was delivered up because of our offences, and was raised up because of our being declared righteous.*"

Explain clearly that Christ was delivered up for man's offenses and bore the judgment that was ours because He had been completely identified with us. He was all that we were, and this identification was so complete that Jesus could not be raised from His condition as our sin-substitute until we could be declared righteous. Use here 1 Timothy 3:16: He was justified or declared righteous. Show this person who has been so indifferent to Christ that he has as much a legal right to righteousness as God's own Son because God, in His love, made His Son sin and that Son couldn't be declared righteous until God had declared man righteous.

When you have reached this stage, point the following fact to the individual with whom you are dealing. Ask him to be honest with himself in considering the issue. His indifference to the Word of God, or his desire to believe that there is not a personal God, is most likely due to the fact that he has within himself consciousness that if there is a God, he cannot stand uncondemned in His presence and has no grounds of approach to Him.

He has been indifferent toward the existence of God and a future life because he has been afraid of God. Then show him that he has a legal right to become the very righteousness of God by personally accepting Christ. He may be freed from all sense of guilt in the presence of God.

MAN'S LEGAL RIGHT TO SONSHIP AND ITS PRIVILEGES

After you have made clear to the one his right to righteousness, show to him on the basis of that his legal right to become a son of God. When a man accepts the redemptive work of Christ on his behalf, he is declared righteous. That is, he stands before God as free from sin as though Adam had never sinned.

He has then the authority to become a child of God. He has the same right to become a child of God that Adam had and forfeited by his crime of high treason.

More than that, he has the same right to become a child of God that Christ had. For Christ had to be born out of spiritual death into eternal life as much as any man today needs to be born again before he can enter the kingdom of heaven. (See John 3:3.)

God has made His Son absolutely one with us, and He had to be born out of spiritual death when He had paid man's penalty. When God raised Christ from the dead, He said to Him, *"Thou art my Son; this day have I begotten thee"* (Psalm 2:7; see also Acts 13:33).

Christ was the first man to be born out of spiritual death into eternal life. (See Hebrews 1:5; Romans 8:29.) We were identified with Him and on the basis of Christ's being born out of Satan's dominion into God's life, every man living has a right to become a Son of God and a joint heir with Christ.

In showing one his identification with Christ, make it as personal as possible. Make him see that God has no favorites. All that Christ did, He did for him as fully as He did it for anyone.

Explain that no man's life is more precious to God than his. Use John 1:12. He has the authority to become a child of God by receiving Christ. Show the one with whom you are dealing the privileges of a child of God that will be his on this earth and also in the new heaven and earth. You may use the following Scriptures: John 17:23; Romans 8:14–17; John 16:23–24; Philippians 4:19; 1 Corinthians 1:30; 1 Peter 5:7.

By presenting, tenderly and sincerely, the legal rights that God has given to man by the sacrifice of His Son, you should be able to arouse every indifferent person you meet and bring many of them to a definite decision for Christ. Master these truths until you will be able to clearly present them, as briefly or fully as the occasion permits, to the ones for whom Christ died who are indifferent towards Him.

Explain to him that Satan has blinded his mind so that the light of the gospel has not entered, for this is the only means that Satan has to keep a man from becoming a child of God. God has legally freed every man from Satan's authority and given him legal rights.

QUESTIONS

1. Name the legal rights that every man possesses.

2. How would you explain to an unsaved man his right to righteousness?

3. Why is it important to show man his right to righteousness?

4. Why does an unsaved man have the right to become a child of God?

10

DEALING WITH THOSE WHO HAVE DIFFICULTIES

We have studied how to deal with those who are indifferent toward accepting Christ. We shall now study how to deal with the class of people who are not indifferent, but are kept from accepting Christ by difficulties.

We shall take up the study of how to meet these individual problems and what Scriptures to use for each one. In meeting problems, we must depend upon the Word for the solution.

"I would accept Christ, but I know that I cannot live a Christian life."

In this lesson, we shall deal with this difficulty; studying how to meet different problems that we face in endeavoring to lead to Christ those who have this reason for not accepting Him as Savior and Lord.

First of all, show the one who has this difficulty that in his condition of spiritual death, he cannot judge his ability to live as a child of God.

Explain to him that it is perfectly natural for him to feel that he cannot live a Christian life because as one who is alienated from God, he would have no love for Him or desire to do His will.

Make it plain to him that when he accepts Christ, he will become a new creation in Christ.

Read to him, if possible, 2 Corinthians 5:17. This will show him that when he accepts Jesus as his Savior and Lord, spiritual death will be eradicated from his spirit and with that eradication, old things will pass away—old desires of selfishness, bitterness, and hatred, and old habits that have held him in bondage.

Use such Scriptures as John 5:24 and 1 John 5:12 to show him that in the place of spiritual death that has reigned in his spirit, he will receive the nature of God. With this nature will come into his life new desires, a definite knowledge of God, a love for God and man, and freedom from sin.

There are many other Scriptures that you may give to the one who is troubled this way. A very important one is Hebrews 7:25. Show him that the Word declares that Christ is able to save him to the uttermost because He ever lives to make intercession for him.

Explain to him that when he becomes a child of God, Christ takes him over and becomes responsible for him. He has been entrusted with our salvation and He is enabled to do it.

To one who has this difficulty, you must make clear the present ministry of Christ.

Among those troubled with this sense of weakness, we will meet those who are afraid of the power of sin.

Give to them Romans 6:14, explaining why children of God are not in bondage to sin. Use also 1 John 4:4, letting him know that the One in him will be greater than the one in the world who has the power of sin.

You will meet those who are *afraid of failure.*

Give to them Jude 1:24, which shows that Christ is able to keep them from falling. Use also 1 Corinthians 10:13 to show them that no great temptation can cause them to fall.

We will also meet in this group those who are bound by a *sense of weakness*.

Show him that the Word declares that his weakness is God's opportunity to manifest His strength. God knows every weakness of the human life and yet He declares that His grace is sufficient, that His strength will be made manifest in human weakness, regardless of what it may be.

The Scripture that meets this problem is 2 Corinthians 12:9–10. You may also be able to use Philippians 4:13 to show that in Christ, he will be able to do all things. Make real to him the fact that when a man becomes a new creation in Christ, Christ's strength takes the place of weakness.

There are those who say, "The Christian life is *too hard*."

Explain that it *would* seem hard to the one who has not become a child of God. Make clear to him that Christianity is not a religion, a set of creeds or doctrines that we try to follow, but it is merely a man's life and walk with God as his Father.

Show him that it is a normal, natural life with God as Father, the normal realm for every man.

Explain to him that when a man has received the life of God and come to a definite knowledge of Him as Father, it is a joy to do His will and doing His will is the essence of the Christian's life.

Scriptures that you may use are: 1 John 5:3; Matthew 11:30; Proverbs 3:17; and Psalm 26:2.

Use Proverbs 13:15 to show him that it is really the life alienated from God that is unnatural and a hard life for man.

In dealing with these individual problems, you must be able to meet them with the Word of God. Therefore, carefully study these Scriptures. If you are not able to memorize each one, memorize its reference so that you will be able to use it quickly and efficiently when the need arises.

In your personal work as you meet difficulties, use the name of Jesus. We are not warring against flesh and blood. (See Ephesians 6:12.)

Always hold the following facts in mind:

+ *"Greater is he that is in you, than he that is in the world"* (1 John 4:4).

+ The reasons that a man has for rejecting Christ are born of the spiritual darkness that blinds his mind. (See 2 Corinthians 4:4.)

+ You have authority in the name of Jesus that is greater than the one who blinds the minds of the unbelieving. (See Mark 16:17.)

Therefore, confidently and with assurance, meet the difficulties with His Word, silently taking deliverance in the name of Jesus from the blindness of Satan over their minds.

Our ability to efficiently and effectively meet the individual problems of those we meet with the Word of God is a big factor in personal work. The lordship of Satan has been legally broken over a man's life. The moment that any man will believe upon Christ, the authority of Satan over his life comes to an end.

Satan has no legal right to have any dominion over man if that man will accept the lordship of Christ.

Therefore, Satan's only means of holding one within his authority is blinding a man to the Word. He blinds a man by presenting him with these difficulties. Therefore, as ambassadors on behalf of Christ, we must prepare to meet these problems with God's Word.

In our next lesson, we will take up other difficulties that we shall encounter. Study each problem carefully and prepare to satisfactorily answer it in your own mind.

QUESTIONS

1. What should be shown to a man who believes that he cannot lead a Christian life?

2. How would you deal with one who is afraid of failure after he becomes a Christian?

3. What Scriptures would you use for one who is afraid of the power of sin?

4. Show how you would help the one who said, "The Christian life is too hard."

5. Why must we be prepared to meet difficulties with the Word of God?

11

DEALING WITH THOSE WHO ARE UNWILLING TO BECOME CHRISTIAN

Winning souls to Christ is the most important work that we have to do. It is the work that is dearest to the heart of the Master. It is really taking His place among men.

To become an efficient soul winner should be our goal. We must prepare ourselves to meet the personal problems and difficulties of those whom we shall endeavor to win to Christ.

Therefore, we are taking up further difficulties that we may meet in our personal work contacts. We want to be prepared to meet every difficulty with His Word, for it is the sword of the Spirit. (See Ephesians 6:17.)

Our wrestling is with *"the rulers of the darkness of this world, against spiritual wickedness in high places"* (Ephesians 6:12).

Behind each difficulty that keeps a man from accepting Christ are the forces of Satan. If we are not prepared to meet these difficulties with God's Word, we cripple the working of the Holy Spirit through us. We hinder His using His sword, the Word of

God, to cast down every thought and every reasoning that exalts itself against the knowledge of Christ. (See 2 Corinthians 10:5.)

Meditate carefully on these Scriptures.

In our last lesson, we dealt, more or less, with difficulties that arose from a sense of an inability to live a Christian life.

In this lesson, we shall take up a different type of difficulties, those that arise more from *an unwillingness to become a Christian.*

FEAR OF PERSECUTION

There are those who do not want to accept Christ because they will be persecuted. When we meet this difficulty, we must not try to eradicate it by telling the inquirer that he will not be persecuted. Instead, we should endeavor to show him that every persecution will bring a reward.

Explain that in the midst of persecution, he will have an inner joy and peace that nothing can destroy. Use Romans 8:18 to show that every suffering for the name of Christ here will be outweighed in glory over there. Also show that in every persecution, His grace will be sufficient for us.

Scriptures that you may use in meeting this difficulty are the following: 2 Timothy 2:12; 3:12; Hebrews 12:2–3; Matthew 5:10–12; and Acts 14:22.

FEAR OF GIVING UP TOO MUCH

A very common difficulty that we shall meet is the feeling that becoming a Christian means giving up too much.

There are those who are unwilling to give up the pleasures of the world for Christ. This is the general attitude of the world toward Him. There are several ways in which we may meet this problem. One way is to show the one with whom you are dealing that to gain the whole world would profit him nothing if he should lose his soul. Use Mark 8:35–37.

Show him that he is an eternal spirit being.

You may also show him that it is perfectly natural for him to have that feeling. In his alienated condition from God, he is dependent upon the world for his happiness. Explain to him the difference between happiness and joy. Happiness comes from without; it is dependent upon favorable circumstances. When the circumstances of one's life change and become unfavorable, happiness leaves. Joy comes from within; it comes from God. It is not dependent upon circumstances.

The world has no joy to give; its best offer is happiness, and when circumstances become contrary, it has no substitute.

Show him that when he becomes a Christian, *"he is a new creature: old things are passed away"* (2 Corinthians 5:17). Old habits and desires will pass away. Explain that all things become new; a new life is his with new joys, new realities.

Show him that nothing that a man gives up can be compared to what he gains in becoming a child of God.

Ask him of what in all the world over may be compared to a definite, positive knowledge of God and a walk in fellowship and communion with Him as Father.

Explain the Father fact of God, the Father's place He will hold in our lives, and His Father love for us. He is interested in our joy and happiness. He would not ask us to give up anything that would be best for our well-being.

Stress here that Christianity is not a set of creeds or doctrines; it is not a religion. It is a Father and His family.

Point out prayer privileges, freedom from anxiety and worry, and the advantages that come from a life with a God of love.

You may use the following Scriptures to bring out those truths: John 1:12; 14:27; 16:27; and Romans 8:28, 31–32.

BUSINESS PROBLEMS

There are those who are unwilling to accept Christ because of business problems.

Some feel that in their business positions, they could not live a Christian life. Others feel that it would hinder their success in business if they were to become Christians.

The first thing to show one who feels that he could not continue in his present business if he were to accept Christ is the fact that it is better to give up an illegitimate business than to lose his soul. Mark 8:35–37 may also be used here.

Then stress the following fact: no legitimate business will ever be hindered by one's accepting Christ and following Him. Show that becoming a Christian is becoming a partner with God.

Use John 14:23. The Father and the Master will live with us in our homes, our businesses, and in all we do.

The miracle-working God will meet every financial need, carry every burden. He has promised to meet every need. (See Philippians 4:19.)

Show the sacredness of His Word to Him, the fact that it cannot be broken, and the utter financial security of the one who will walk with Him. You may also use Matthew 6:33. Righteousness is the ability to walk with God without a sense of guilt or condemnation.

One of the results of seeking His righteousness is the ability to walk fearlessly, trusting Him.

FEAR OF LOSING FRIENDS

There are those who are unwilling to accept Christ because they will lose friends.

Show this group the rich fellowship and loving friendship that springs up between those who become brothers and sisters of Christ.

Show the close tie of love between members of God's family and joint-heirs with Jesus Christ, the mutual burden-bearing and care for one another.

Explain that this love for each other, the Father, and Jesus is the very heart of Christianity.

You may use John 13:33–34; Romans 15:1; and 1 Corinthians 12:25–26.

QUESTIONS

1. If we are not prepared to meet personal difficulties with the Word, what effect will it have upon our ministry?

2. Tell how to answer the one who is afraid of persecution for Christ's sake.

3. How would you deal with the one who felt that becoming a Christian meant giving up too much?

4. Explain how to show an unsaved man that becoming a Christian would not harm his business.

5. What truths would you give to one who did not want to accept Christ because he would lose friends by doing so?

12

DEALING WITH THOSE WHO HAVE LOST HOPE

We have studied two classes of difficulties: those that arise from a sense of an inability to live a Christian life and those that arise from an unwillingness to become a Christian.

We shall now study how to deal with another type of problem. There are difficulties that we shall meet in our personal work arising from a sense of hopelessness. How many there are who have lost all hope of ever becoming a child of God! We shall now study some of the individual problems that we shall meet in this group.

UNABLE TO FIND CHRIST

There are a large number of people who have been seeking Christ for a long period of time and are seemingly unable to find Him.

Many, because of this, have become quite hopeless. Their difficulty is usually due to the fact that they have mistaken mental assent for faith.

The personal worker, in order to be successful, must understand the difference between mental assent and faith. An understanding of mental assent and knowing how to deal with it will enable him to help not only a great number who are seeking salvation, but also a great number who need healing or a victorious life in Christ.

Mental assent is consenting to the fact that the Bible is true and professing to believe it, but that profession is void of action. It means nothing to the Father.

"Faith, if it hath not works, is dead" (James 2:17). A better translation might be, "Faith, if it does not have corresponding actions, is dead." In other words, it is mental assent, not faith.

A professing faith that will not stand upon the Word of God and act fearlessly upon it, regardless of feeling or circumstances, is only mental assent. A man is born again by faith in the Word of God. He is not born again by mental assent. He is begotten of the Word of God when he acts upon it and makes it his confession.

> For by grace are ye saved through faith; and that not of your-
> selves: it is the gift of God.   (Ephesians 2:8)

The moment that a man believes, he receives the life of God. The new birth is God's Word. It is God who imparts His nature to the spirit of man.

When a man has believed, the rest is up to God. *"We are his workmanship, created in Christ Jesus unto good works"* (Ephesians 2:10).

Many say, "I have believed, but I am not saved." They have not believed, for believing has a positive confession.

The following incident will illustrate this truth. One evening, I was speaking with a woman who had remained after the service for those who were seeking Christ.

She was weeping bitterly. She said, "For six months, I have been seeking Christ. It is so hard to be saved."

I gave to her Revelation 3:20, showing her that Christ was asking to come into her life, and that when she invited Him in, He came. I also gave her John 5:24, showing that the moment she believed in His Word, she had eternal life.

She said, "I believe, but I am not saved. I do believe. I have believed the Bible all my life."

She was not believing, however. Believing is acting upon the Word of God. Believing is confessing that what God says, is. If she had believed, she would have said, "I have invited Jesus into my life. Therefore, He has come in because His Word declares so."

For six months, she had been only mentally assenting. She had been assenting to the fact that the Bible is the Word of God, yet there was no action, no positive confession. Mental assent has no conception of the sacredness of God's Word. Faith is satisfied with the evidence of the Word of God alone.

I had this inquirer read Revelation 3:20 and John 5:24 aloud over and over again. As she read, I explained to her that it is impossible for God's Word to fail, that the integrity of the Word was the integrity of God. The Word began to work in her life. She stepped from the realm of mental assent into the realm of faith.

Suddenly, she laughed and said, "It is so simple. I believe; therefore I have eternal life." When she acted upon the Word of God, then God made it good and imparted to her His own nature.

In your personal work, you will find many who have gone to the altar several times without finding Christ.

To those, you must show the difference between mental assent and faith. Show them that they must take God at His Word. Seek to bring them to a knowledge of the sacredness of God's Word to Himself.

You may illustrate this by an example of the sacredness of the word of an honest man.

If we lose faith in a man's word, we have lost faith in him. An honest man will be careful of his words. He will not promise that which he cannot perform. He will watch over his word to make it good in every case.

Show that it is only through God's Word that man can know Him. Therefore, it is sacred, for if it fails, He fails.

Use Jeremiah 1:12 to show that God is watching over His Word to perform it in the life of the man or woman who will act upon it. Show the inquirer that he must not wait for a feeling of salvation before he confesses that he is saved. Explain that the joy of the Christian does not come necessarily at the moment he is born again, but from his fellowship with the Father.

Show him that greater than the evidence of feelings or experiences is the evidence of God's Word, which declares that when a man believes, he has eternal life (see John 5:24), or that when he invites Christ in, He comes in.

Mental assent is one of the weapons that Satan uses to hinder those who are anxious to be saved. It is dangerous and subtle because it is clothed in the term "faith." The seeker does not realize that it is *not* faith and cannot analyze his difficulty in not finding Christ as his Savior and Lord.

As personal workers, we must be prepared to destroy mental assent and build faith in its place through the Word. *"Faith cometh by hearing, and hearing by the word of God"* (Romans 10:17).

FEAR THAT IT'S TOO LATE

There are those who have lost hope because of the feeling that it is too late. Many have previously rejected Christ and feel that, because of that rejection, God will not receive them.

The need of this group can be met by building the Word into their lives so that they will come to a place of action upon it.

Many times, their attitude is only one of mental assent toward the great promises of God's Word that would bring life to them.

Use 2 Peter 3:9 to show that it is not God's will for any man to perish. John 6:37 is a good Scripture for this group as it shows that Christ will receive whosoever comes unto Him at any time.

God declares, *"Whosoever shall call upon the name of the Lord shall be saved"* (Romans 10:13). Other Scriptures to be used are Deuteronomy 4:30–31; Isaiah 1:18; and Revelation 22:17.

QUESTIONS

1. What is the usual difficulty of those who have been seeking Christ for a long time without finding Him?

2. Distinguish between mental assent and faith.

3. Explain how to deal with a mental assenter.

4. Why is mental assent so dangerous?

5. Show how to deal with a man who felt that it was too late to be saved.

13

DEALING WITH THOSE WHO HAVE FALSE HOPES

In our last lesson, we studied the methods whereby we could deal with those who had a sense of hopelessness and those who felt that they could not become children of God.

In our efforts for the Master, we shall very often contact another group of people whose need is the opposite. They refuse to seriously consider the acceptance of Christ as their Savior because they are entertaining false hopes for their own salvation.

In the place of hopelessness, they have too many hopes. A large number of people belong to this group. We are contacting them continually. Some of the finest people we know belong to this number. They assent to the existence of God and a future life, yet they are without concern for their soul's welfare. A great body of church members, nominal Christians, belong to this class. We must be prepared to teach them.

Perhaps the largest number of this class are those who expect to be *saved by their works of righteousness*. These people believe that they are not sinners. They say they are doing the best they can in doing unto others as they would have done unto them.

They believe that through their honest and moral lives, they have as much right to enter heaven as anyone.

Many of the Scriptures and facts that we studied in dealing with the indifferent would help in this class.

The greatest fact to make clear to those who expect to be saved by what they are doing is the following:

+ A man does not enter heaven because of what he does (right living), nor is he refused admittance into heaven because of what he does (wrong living). A man enters heaven because of what he is through the new birth—a child of God.

+ A man is refused entrance into heaven because of what he is by nature, a child of wrath. (See Ephesians 2:3.)

Their need may be met, if they are honest in their opinion of salvation by their own works, by showing them the message God has given to us in the book of Romans.

The book of Romans is a legal document. It is revelation brought down to the light of human reason so that an unsaved man may understand it. The first three chapters are a courthouse scene.

In the first chapter, the gentile world is brought before the judgment throne of God. The judgment comes from Him that His wrath is revealed against their unrighteousness.

For the wrath of God is revealed from heaven against all ungodliness and unrighteousness of men, who hold the truth in unrighteousness.   (Romans 1:18)

In the second chapter, the Jew is brought before God and the same indictment is brought against them. He says that, through their inability to keep the law, the name of God has been blasphemed among the gentiles. (See Romans 2:24.)

The conclusion from the throne of God is given in Romans 3:9–10: "*What then? are we* [Jews] *better than they* [Gentiles]? *No, in no wise: for we have before proved both Jews and Gentiles, that they are all under sin; as it is written, There is none righteous, no, not one.*"

No unsaved man stands righteous before God because he is "*under sin*"—under the sin of Adam that brought spiritual death, the nature of Satan.

Study Romans 5:12–21 so that you will be able to expound upon it to an unsaved person.

Then show how God continues by showing that nothing that a man can do will make him righteous. (See Romans 3:20.) You may use for an illustration of this fact the example of the failure of the Jew to become righteous by his own efforts through the law. His failure was due to the fact that he was spiritually dead, a child of Satan.

However, never try to make a man see his need of Christ and His righteousness by pointing out to him that he is under the curse of the law as long as he trusts in his own works. Many teachers teach this, but it is wrong, for the gentile was not given the law. It was given to the Jew; no gentile has ever come under the law except through circumcision. The gentile's position is shown in Ephesians 2:12 (TCNT): "*You were shut out from the citizenship of Israel; you were strangers to the Covenants founded on God's Promise; you were in the world without hope and without God.*"

Continue with Romans 3:21–30 to show that God has provided a righteousness for man through faith in Christ. Use 2 Corinthians 5:21 to show how He has done it.

In the past lessons, we have covered how to show an inquirer the way of the new birth and the righteousness that becomes man's through faith in Christ, so we will not deal with it now.

If you, through meditation and prayer, will let these passages of Scripture master you, the Holy Spirit will be able to use you effectually in showing a man who is honest with himself salvation through faith in Christ alone.

Others who entertain false hopes are those who say, "A God of love would not send anyone to hell." We can meet this by explaining that we know nothing of God's love except through the Bible, and the Bible teaches plainly the existence of heaven and hell. The whole message of redemption, the reason for Christ's coming, centers in the fact that hell became the eternal home of man through Adam's high treason.

God does not send a man to hell. Man goes to hell because he is a child of Satan. If he continues in this life as a child of Satan, he will remain one with him after death, which means that he must go to his father's home.

God has provided a redemption in Christ whereby a man may come out of Satan's kingdom (see Colossians 1:13) into Christ's kingdom and become a child of God. (See John 1:12.)

When a man becomes a child of God, heaven becomes his home as logically and naturally as hell becomes the home of the child of Satan.

Show that God has done all that He can to save a man from hell. He cannot, however, go beyond man's will. A man wills to remain alienated from God, or he wills to become a child of God.

Christ said, *"If any man will do his will, he shall know of the doctrine, whether it be of God, or whether I speak of myself"* (John 7:17). If a man wills to know these things, he will know.

Others say, "I feel that I am all right. I am not afraid to die. I feel that I will go to heaven."

We can show these that we only know of heaven and a future life through the revelation that God has given to us. Jesus said, *"No man cometh unto the Father, but by me"* (John 14:6).

God hath given to us eternal life, and this life is in his Son.
He that hath the Son hath life; and he that hath not the Son of
God hath not life.   (1 John 5:11–12)

He that believeth on the Son hath everlasting life: and he that
believeth not the Son shall not see life; but the wrath of God
abideth on him.   (John 3:36)

A man has no authority for faith in his feelings alone. A man may know definitely that he will go to heaven when his faith is resting on God's Word.

QUESTIONS

1.   What is the greatest fact to make clear to a man who expects to be saved by his own works?

2.   Show how you would expound the message of Romans in meeting the above need.

3.   How would you deal with one who believed that a God of love would not send anyone to hell?

4.   What would you show the one who said, "I feel all right"?

5.   Did you carefully study every Scripture in the lesson?

14

BROKEN FELLOWSHIP

There is a great need today in the church for an understanding of broken fellowship. As personal workers, we must be qualified to efficiently deal with those who have broken fellowship with the Father.

Fellowship is the very heart of Christianity, yet little is known or taught about it in the churches. We have only known it as *backsliding*, but backsliding and backsliders are incorrect terms. They are not scriptural. We should never use them.

A person does not backslide from the new birth. He loses his fellowship with the Father and his Master. Few have known the distinction between relationship and fellowship. A man who has broken fellowship has not necessarily lost his relationship. Fellowship is easily broken by us, yet only God can break up our relationship.

One cannot annul his own marriage. The law that married a man must unmarry him. However, a couple may destroy their fellowship and wreck the joy of marriage.

The most important thing in human and divine relationship is to maintain fellowship.

So little has been understood about it that many have broken their fellowship and call themselves *backsliders,* considering themselves as lost.

They do not realize how quickly and easily their relationship may be restored.

There are two classes of those who are out of fellowship. One class includes those who have no desire to come back to the Father. This is usually due to the fact that they have never really known the joy that comes from the fullness of fellowship with the Father and His Son.

"Truly our fellowship is with the Father, and with his Son Jesus Christ" (1 John 1:3). The chief joy of the Christian lies in fellowship with God. If the fellowship is rich and strong, then faith becomes healthy and robust.

Many who have been born again have not been taught their place in Christ. They do not understand their privileges in Him. Many who have broken fellowship have never known their place as actual sons and daughters of God. (See 1 John 3:1; Romans 8:14–17.) They did not know that they have become the righteousness of God.

They did not know that in Christ, they were free from the dominion of sin and Satan. (See Romans 6:10; Hebrews 2:14.)

Nothing has caused children of God to lose fellowship more quickly than ignorance of the Word of God. *"My people are destroyed for lack of knowledge"* (Hosea 4:6).

God's children have lived in broken fellowship because they have been destroyed by lack of knowledge of the Word. No one would desire to continue in broken fellowship if he knew what his privileges in Christ were.

Sin would not keep him in broken fellowship, for sin is no longer a problem to God's child. It has been put away in Christ.

To one who is afraid of the power of sin over his life, Hebrews 9:26 shows that sin has been adequately met and destroyed through redemption. It originated in Satan, but he has been brought to naught as far as the new creation is concerned. (See Hebrews 2:14.)

Show to the one who has no desire to come back into fellowship what he is forfeiting: a walk upon earth with all the privileges and joys of an actual child of God, and the Father's care and protection over his life.

There are certain Scriptures that you may use in your personal work with this group as the Holy Spirit leads you: Jeremiah 2:19; Proverbs 14:14; 1 Kings 11:9; and Luke 15:13–17.

The other class of people who are living in broken fellowship are those who desire to come back to the Father but do not know how.

Show to this group that they have not broken their relationship, but their fellowship. They are still God's children. Their condition is described in 1 John 1:5–10. In their condition of broken fellowship, they are walking in darkness, and they are not without sin.

However, God's redemption in Christ has made provision for them. They have an advocate with the Father. *"If any man sin, we have an advocate with the Father, Jesus Christ the righteous"* (1 John 2:1).

Although they have lost their standing, there is One in heaven who is there for them, on their behalf.

He is on an equality with God. He is security for them. They may have their fellowship restored instantly by confessing their condition and asking forgiveness.

Many here will say, "I have done that. I ask Him continually to forgive me." Here the difficulty lies in the fact that they are mentally assenting to the Word.

You must bring them to a point of action upon it. Show them that the Word, which declares that they are in darkness and with sin, declares that the moment they confess their sins, they are forgiven and cleansed from all unrighteousness. You must point out to them that what God says is, regardless of their feelings.

The moment they confess their sins, God forgives them and forgets them. Show them that "believing" is thanking the Father for forgiveness, and forgetting the past. The Father forgets what He has forgiven. We must forget it too.

Use Luke 15:11–24, the story of the prodigal son, to show the attitude of the Father toward His child who has been living in broken fellowship and the glad way in which He receives him back.

The real need of this group is to be brought from the realm of mental assent into the realm of action upon the Word of God.

Have them read this Scripture aloud until it works in their lives:

> *If we confess our sins, he is faithful and just to forgive us our sins, and to cleanse us from all unrighteousness.* (1 John 1:9)

This is God's remedy for broken fellowship. No one need remain in broken fellowship any longer than it takes to ask forgiveness.

There are many Scriptures that reveal the readiness of the Father to receive those who have been living in broken fellowship.

In the old covenant, we see in many Scriptures God's tenderness manifested toward Israel at times when they had broken their fellowship. At times, the Holy Spirit may lead you to use these: Hosea 14:1–4; Jeremiah 27:11–13; Jeremiah 3:13, 22; Isaiah 43:22–25; Isaiah 44:20–22; Deuteronomy 4:28–31; and 2 Chronicles 7:14.

After showing one how to restore his fellowship, always give to him instructions for the maintenance of fellowship.

In our next lesson, we shall study instructions that should be given to the one who has just become a child of God, for his walk with the Father.

These instructions will be the same ones that we may give to those who have restored their fellowship with the Father and the Master.

QUESTIONS

1. Why should we never use the terms "backslider" or "backsliding"?

2. Show the difference between *relationship* and *fellowship*.

3. What are the two classes of those who are living in broken fellowship?

4. What would you show to one who has no desire to restore his fellowship?

5. How would you deal with one who said, "I have asked Him to forgive me many times"?

15

INSTRUCTIONS TO GIVE TO THOSE YOU HAVE LED TO CHRIST

In our last lesson, we studied how to deal with those who had broken fellowship with the Father.

A large number of those who find Christ in evangelistic services lose fellowship with the Father afterwards because sufficient instructions from God's Word were not given to them.

Never leave a person whom you have led to Christ without clearly instructing him as to his place in Christ.

These instructions must also be given to one whose fellowship has been restored, that he might know how to maintain that fellowship.

If, at the time when you lead one to Christ, time will not permit your giving these instructions, if possible, visit the person or endeavor to contact him that you may instruct him in the Christian life.

Follow-up work is very important. Whenever it is possible, always keep in contact with those who have been born again through your ministry.

There are three main points that we should cover in the instructions that we give to the new man in Christ. Hold these three factors in your mind and endeavor to cover them sufficiently and clearly. The three phases are:

1. Show him his place in Christ.

2. Show him how to meet temptation.

3. Show him how to maintain his fellowship with the Father and the Master.

After you have led a man to Christ, show him what he has become through his action upon the Word of God.

A knowledge of what God has made us at the new birth does not come to us through our emotions. It comes through the Word alone.

The first need of the one who has been born again is the renewing of his mind. When a man becomes God's child, his spirit receives the life of God.

His mind, which had been darkened, blinded, and controlled by spiritual death, must be renewed by God's Word.

Be not conformed to this world: but be ye transformed by the renewing of your mind.   (Romans 12:2)

Be renewed in the spirit of your mind.   (Ephesians 4:23)

A man's mind is renewed as he learns of what he is in Christ. The renewing of his mind should begin at the moment he is born again.

Show the one who has been born again just what has taken place in his life.

Use Colossians 1:13 to show him that he has been taken out of the realm of spiritual death, Satan's family, into the realm of life, God's family.

Explain that his spirit has received the nature of God (see 2 Peter 1:4) and he has become an actual child of God and joint-heir with Jesus Christ. (See Romans 8:14–17.)

Use John 17:23 to show that the Father loves him as He loves Christ.

Use 2 Corinthians 5:21 and 1 Corinthians 1:30 to show him his standing before God.

Show him his privileges of prayer as given in John 14:13–14; 15:7; and 16:23–24.

Satanic forces will attack the newborn babe in Christ, so explain to him the spiritual warfare that is arrayed against us.

For we wrestle not against flesh and blood, but against principalities, against powers, against the rulers of the darkness of this world, against spiritual wickedness in high places.

(Ephesians 6:12)

However, make clear that these are conquered enemies and cannot defeat us. Use Hebrews 2:14 and Ephesians 1:21–23.

Satan may attack us through temptations, but show the one with whom you are dealing, definitely and positively, how to be free from sin's dominion.

For this purpose use Romans 6:6–11. Explain that every attack of the adversary is met by the Word. If he will stand upon the Word of God, making it his confession in times of temptation, sin cannot have dominion over him, for its power has been broken through Christ.

Explain that every temptation is a bluff of the adversary.

It is also very important to give instructions for the maintenance of fellowship.

In this, reading and meditation in God's Word cannot be stressed too highly.

Broken fellowship always arises if one stops feeding upon the Word. The Scriptures are our Father's message to us. It is the food for our spirit. We live by it. *"Man doth not live by bread only, but by every word that proceedeth out of the mouth of the Lord"* (Deuteronomy 8:3; see also Matthew 4:4). It works in our lives, building us up, and making us strong in Him. (See 1 Thessalonians 2:13.)

In order to maintain a high type of fellowship, time must be set aside daily for a study of the Word and prayer, communion with the Father and the Master.

Always stress the importance of testimony. Use Revelation 12:11. Our growth may be measured largely by the strength and frequency of our confession of Him.

The present ministry of Christ must also be shown. Many are prone to consider that Christ's ministry for us ended at the time that He arose from the dead and ascended to the Father.

Explain that Christ's ministry did not end then, but that it merely became enlarged. Christ is giving Himself for us and is living for us today in as much reality as He did when He died for us.

It is very necessary to explain Christ's ministry as our Advocate:

If we confess our sins, he is faithful and just to forgive us our sins, and to cleanse us from all unrighteousness. (1 John 1:9)

If any man sin, we have an advocate with the Father, Jesus Christ the righteous: and he is the propitiation for our sins: and not for ours only, but also for the sins of the whole world.
(1 John 2:1–2)

Many times, Satan causes us to stumble, to say and do things that break our fellowship with the Father and the Master.

Explain that if he does fail, or break his fellowship, he need remain in that condition no longer than it takes to ask forgiveness.

Many break their fellowship and continue on in it, the breach becoming greater because they do not know that Christ is man's Advocate, praying for him at the Father's right hand.

We have given here a great deal of material and many Scriptures. Your reading this lesson through once will not equip you to successfully instruct the new man in Christ. You must study it carefully until these truths and Scriptures master you.

Perhaps you will not have time to give all of these truths to the individuals with whom you are dealing. However, give as much of it as you can. Perhaps it will take several conversations to cover it.

Of course, the one to whom you are giving these Scriptures cannot remember them all. Therefore, always carry with you a small notebook and paper and be ready to write for him the references of all the Scriptures that you give to him.

You will find that you may give these instructions not only to those who have just become Christians, or to those who have restored broken fellowship, but also to those who are living defeated Christian lives.

QUESTIONS

1. Why do many who are saved in evangelistic services never go on?

2. After you have led one to Christ, what is your responsibility toward him?

3. What would you give to show the new Christian his place in Christ?

4. How would you show one his victory over sin?

5. What instructions would you use to show one how to maintain his fellowship with the Father and Master?

16

DEALING WITH THE SKEPTICAL

Today the average man has no concern for his personal responsibility toward God.

He does not consider the Bible to be God's Word. He places it upon the same level as the sacred writings of other ancient peoples.

He gives it no more value than he would a group of myths because he believes it contains scientific error.

There are many Christians who brush the difficulty aside. They say that we do not expect to find theology in a scientific textbook, nor do we expect to find science in a theological book.

This, however, does not solve the difficulty.

Although we do not expect to find science taught to us in a book coming from God, we do not expect to find scientific error in it, for its Author, knowing all things and being Himself the Creator of the universe, could not write through man that which contained blunders on any subject.

Others say that God spoke to man in ancient times and that their minds were so steeped in error that He could not speak to them in the light of the modern era. They say He came down to their level just as a father comes down in his talking to the level of his little boy.

This does not solve the problem either. Although a father does talk to a boy on his own level, he does not need to say anything that could cause the boy in later years to lose faith in his father's integrity.

If the Bible is a revelation from God, it cannot contain scientific error.

In ancient times, God spoke nothing to ancient man that would cause modern man to lose faith in His Word. Let us consider the so-called scientific mistakes of the Bible to see whether or not they are errors after all.

As personal workers, we must be prepared to give a reason to every man who asks concerning the hope that is within us, a hope based upon His Word.

It is growing more precious to us every day. We know that it is God's revelation to us, so we must prepare ourselves to deal with those whom we may meet who sincerely believe that the Bible contains scientific error.

LIGHT BEFORE THE SUN

We commonly hear today of the mistakes of Moses, especially in reference to the first chapter of Genesis.

The fact that in the history of creation in Genesis 1:3, we have light before and seemingly without the sun seems an erroneous statement to many.

However, science now teaches that light is not dependent upon the sun for its existence.

Light is the result of force causing the waves of ether to vibrate with an almost infinite rapidity.

We can measure the greatness of that force by the fact that light travels around the earth eight times a second.

We find in Genesis 1:2 that the first thing that took place in creation was that the Holy Spirit *"moved upon the face of the waters."*

The word "moved" in Hebrew is a continuative verb meaning "kept moving." We have here the introduction and continuation of the force and the result was light.

Since the invention of photography, the ideas of scientists upon the subject of light have been revolutionized. The action of light on the plates has shown that it was one of the greatest forces in the universe, and that its action was necessary to prepare the way for all life.

This knowledge about light was one of the greatest scientific discoveries made at the close of the nineteenth century, yet is was written in the Bible thirty-four centuries ago.

ANTIQUITY OF MAN

Another so-called error of the Bible is the fact that Bible chronology gives about 6,000 years as the span of man's existence upon the globe.

We know that man's arrival was preceded by an ice age. If we knew just when the ice age ended, we should be able to judge fairly accurately the time when the first man appeared.

At first, science gave us 850,000 years as the span. Then James Croll and James Geikie said that 80,000 years had passed since the ice age.

Sir Joseph Prestwich believed it to have ended 20,000 or 30,000 years ago.

So we can see that scientific numbers have been tumbling down in a wholesale fashion toward the number given to us in Bible chronology.

However, these numbers are more or less based upon theory and a more accurate measurement has been used.

Our rivers have ploughed their channels since the ice was cleared away from the surface. Niagara has had to cut through the rock gorge down which it hurls the huge mass of waters that form the falls. It has ploughed out seven miles. Research has revealed that the falls started forming 7,000 to 12,000 years ago.

Thus we can see that the latest scientific knowledge is bringing us down to Bible dates.

These two seeming mistakes of the Bible are some of the "certainties" that have caused people to reject God's Word upon the grounds that it contained scientific error.

If the Bible had given the existence of the sun before light, or the date of man's appearance at a much later date, it might have been in harmony with science of the last century, but present-day science would have proved it untrue.

Many believe that Genesis 1 records the creation of the world in six days.

We have creation in six periods, however, not days of twenty-four hours.

It is evident that these periods were not our days of twenty-four hours each, for the earth did not begin to revolve on its axis around the sun until the fourth period.

Therefore, the days could not be twenty-four hours each. We shall continue this study in our next lesson.

(We wish to add that we are indebted to John Urquhart's *Roger's Reasons, or the Bible and Science* for much of the material in this lesson.)

QUESTIONS

1. What is the attitude of modern man toward the Bible?

2. Why must we as personal workers be prepared to meet those who believe that the Bible contains scientific errors?

3. Explain the existence of light before the sun.

4. Show how science is showing that the Bible is authentic in the date that it gives us for the appearance of man.

5. How would you deal with one who believed that the creation days were twenty-four hours each?

17

DEALING WITH BIBLE VS. SCIENCE SKEPTICS

We are continuing in this lesson a study of the seemingly scientific errors of the Bible.

One of the most common erroneous beliefs we shall meet is the belief that the Bible teaches that the earth is flat. The skeptics in general believe this.

There are several reasons for this common belief. For one, the phrase "ends of the earth" is mentioned in several Scriptures. However, today, in circumstances similar to those in which the Bible used the phrase, we would speak of the phrase "ends of the earth" without calling it a scientific error.

If we wished to express the great distance from which a group of people had come to witness a great event, we might say they had come from "the ends of the earth."

Another reason for believing that the Bible teaches that the earth is flat is found in the terms "foundations" and "pillars" when used in reference to the earth. Many believe that this refers to the fact that the earth is resting as a flat plain upon foundations and pillars. However, these terms apply to the internal arrangements in this planet.

Urquhart tells us that some scientists have judged these expressions to be marvelously accurate in describing how the solid crust of the earth has been built up.

On the other hand, the Bible very definitely teaches us that the earth is round. It taught this at a time when science had not been developed and the common opinion of other nations was that the earth was flat.

We, as personal workers, must prepare ourselves to give these Scriptures to anyone who sincerely believes that the Bible teaches error upon this subject.

The first Scripture that we will use is Job 26:7: *"He…hangeth the earth upon nothing."* This Scripture reveals to us the law of gravitation. The earth is fixed, held in its place, yet it is suspended from nothing. No support reached out to it from any side. A divine operation has placed it and holds it there.

Another Scripture is Isaiah 40:22: *"It is he that sitteth upon the circle of the earth."* The Hebrew word translated "circle" does not mean a circle drawn upon a plain surface, but it means a sphere, in a literal translation. Scripture could not be plainer here in showing to us that the earth is not flat.

Deuteronomy 4:19 also shows in a very clear way that the earth is round: *"Which the LORD thy God hath divided unto all nations under the whole heaven."* God here is warning Israel against following other nations in the worship of the stars.

It is only the light of modern scientific knowledge that enables us to understand this Scripture. God has given to different nations a different portion of the stars. Now, if the earth were a flat plain, all nations would see the same stars, but because it is a globe, different nations see different stars. In the Southern Hemisphere, they do not see the Great Bear or the North Star, but they see the Southern Cross.

Here is another Scripture that very positively shows the earth to be round:

> I tell you, in that night there shall be two men in one bed; the one shall be taken, and the other shall be left. Two women shall be grinding together; the one shall be taken, and the other left. Two men shall be in the field; the one shall be taken, and the other left. (Luke 17:34–36)

Now, note here the fact that Christ said that when He returned, it would be night in one section of Earth, daylight in another, and midday in another. This Scripture can only be understood in the knowledge of the fact that the earth is a sphere revolving around the sun.

The above Scriptures could only have been written through inspiration of the Holy Spirit, for man, at the time when they were written, did not possess this knowledge. In studying the beliefs of any contemporary people at the time each Scripture was written, we find that each one held fantastical and grotesque beliefs about the earth. The Hindus possessed some of the greatest intellects of humanity, yet they believed that the earth rested upon the back of a huge elephant, and this upon a turtle, and so forth.

This belief was similar to the beliefs of other nations at that time.

Another common erroneous attitude of the skeptical toward the Bible is that the Bible gives a wrong impression of the relationship of Earth in size to the heavenly bodies.

It is commonly believed that it magnifies the size of the earth and that it gives the impression that the heavenly bodies are of no greater size and importance than they appear to be. However, this is not true, and we find just the opposite revealed to us.

Let us notice Psalm 8:3–4: "When I consider thy heavens, the work of thy fingers, the moon and the stars, which thou hast ordained;

what is man, that thou art mindful of him? and the son of man, that thou visitest him?"

Now here we have the wonder of modern astronomy.

This Scripture could only have been spoken by inspiration of the Holy Spirit. At the time that this was written, man believed that the sun, the moon, and the stars were of no greater size than they appeared to be to the naked eye. A man with this conception of the heavenly universe could never have the feeling which the psalmist expressed. The psalmist, in considering the greatness of the heavenly bodies and the utter smallness and insignificance of the earth and man in comparison, cries out, *"What is man, that thou art mindful of him?"*

We see here also his wonder and exclamation of awe at the incarnation, which is revealed here, that God should actually visit man upon this small and insignificant planet.

It is clearly seen that a man with the conception of that day of the relationship of the earth to the heavenly universe could not feel the awe of the psalmist expressed here. To him, it would seem perfectly natural that the earth should be considered and even visited by the Creator, for to him, the heavenly universe would be of small significance and importance compared to the earth, which seemed so great to him.

This unutterable majesty of the heavenly universe, as revealed in the Scripture, does not remove God from us. Our contemplation of the greatness of the heavenly bodies reveals to us more the fullness and wonder of His love. Insignificant as Earth is, man was remembered by his Creator, who Himself took the form of a man and visited this planet, becoming sin on our behalf, that man might be reconciled to Him.

QUESTIONS

1. How would you show one that the phrase *ends of the earth* did not indicate that the earth was flat?

2. How would you explain the meaning of the terms "foundations" and "pillars"?

3. Explain Deuteronomy 4:19.

4. Explain Luke 17:34–36.

5. What other Scriptures show that the earth is round?

6. Explain the Scripture that confirms the inspiration of the Holy Spirit in regard to modern astronomy.

18

DEALING WITH BIBLE VS. SCIENCE SKEPTICS (PART 2)

In our learning how to deal with the skeptical, we have been studying the seemingly scientific errors of the Bible. We have found, however, when we analyze them, that they are not really errors.

It is essential for us to realize this and know how to meet this problem, for the general attitude toward the Bible is that it is filled with scientific error.

On the other hand, we find that when we study the Bible carefully, it is not only free from error, but it also presents scientific truths. It sets forth truth that was not known at that time and could only have been written under the inspiration of the Holy Spirit.

Urquhart has analyzed a number of these Scriptures, and we wish to give them to you now, that you might have them to use in case you need them.

Let us take Genesis 1:9: *"And God said, Let the waters under the heaven be gathered together unto one place, and let the dry land appear."* We notice here that the seas were not gathered together into one place, although that is not mentioned about the land. We also note this: though the waters are called seas, they are gathered together into one place.

As a result of our explorations through the centuries, we have discovered the fact that all the seas are connected, and the dry land is segregated. How could any man at the time that this was written have understood that or known it?

Another fact of creation that shows the scriptural account to be correct is that it places man as the last of creation's work. Let us note what geologists have said about this.

Professor James D. Dana, whose name was one of the very biggest in geology, lectured upon the creation story given in Genesis at Yale University several years before he died. He made the statement that inspiration alone could account for its record that was in accord with recent discoveries, mentioning the fact that Professor Arnold H. Guyot, a fellow scientist, had come to the same conclusion. Guyot, a professor of history in a Swiss university, decided to commence with the origin of all things and studied every book that was available on biology, geology, and astronomy. He tabulated his results and found that he had placed the order of events in the same order that was given in the first chapter of Genesis.

Science places the advent of man last in the series, but the Bible proclaimed the truth thousands of years before any investigations had been made.

As we study these Scriptures, we are convinced of the fact that the Holy Spirit must have formed the very statements that were written, for no man could have written with such scientific accuracy.

We notice this is Ecclesiastes 1:7: *"All the rivers run into the sea; yet the sea is not full; unto the place from whence the rivers come, thither they return again."*

This is a positively scientific statement. Hundreds of thousands of tons of water are being poured into the sea every hour of every day and night, but the sea is not full.

The explanation that the Scripture gives to us is that the rivers flow back to the places from which they started. But what man has ever seen them go back, and what man could have made such a statement as a result of his own conclusions? We find the explanation to this Scripture in Psalm 135:7: *"He causeth the vapours to ascend from the ends of the earth; he maketh lightnings for the rain; he bringeth the wind out of his treasuries."* Here is a Scripture that is in perfect harmony with modern science.

Every moment of every day, vapor is rising from the oceans in great volumes and regularity. As the watery vapor is condensed, clouds are formed. If these clouds were left where they were formed, they would fall again into the sea, and it would be filled, but God has made preparations for the earth's needs. He brings *"the wind out of his treasuries"* and these winds bear the clouds back to the coast, yet they have not yet gone back to the places from which they started.

The clouds must become rain, and the Scripture says, *"He maketh lightnings for the rain."* There is one kind of electricity in one cloud and another kind of electricity in another. The contact of the two clouds coming together causes the lightning flash that sends the rain to the earth.

William Thomson, Lord Kelvin, believed there was never rain without lightning. How accurate, therefore, these Scriptures are. The earth is refreshed with the rain. Streams are formed, the springs overflow, the rivers are replenished, and they are swept back again into the ocean.

Let us notice Isaiah 40:12: *"Who hath measured the waters in the hollow of his hand, and meted out heaven with the span, and comprehended the dust of the earth in a measure, and weighed the mountains in scales, and the hills in a balance?"* Every clause here presents a scientific fact.

The implication in the first clause is that God measured a certain quantity of water in the hollow of His hand, and then gave that portion for Earth's water supply.

Science now bears witness to this fact. Our water supply has been measured. It is an exact quantity. We could use no more, and we require no less. If the water surface had been larger than it is now, we would have had too much rain; if it had been any less, we would not have had enough rain to have supported the earth's population.

Water is indispensable, and it is the only natural liquid that exists in a free state at the earth's temperature. A small change in temperature would vaporize or solidify it, which would make it impossible for life to be maintained upon the earth.

Let us take the next clause: *"And meted out heaven with the span."* In other words, He measured the atmosphere and fixed it at a certain height. We know now that the atmosphere above us is of the exact measurement that is required to support life. If the height of the atmosphere were any less or any more, we could not live on Earth.

One constituent of our atmosphere is ozone, which exists miles above the earth in such a small measurement that if it were brought to the surface, it would make a gaseous layer about as thick as a book cover. Yet, if it were not for this portion of ozone in our atmosphere, humanity would meet with blindness or death from the sun's rays.

Notice now the last clause: *"And weighed the mountains in scales, and the hills in a balance."* Physical geography tells us now that the height of the mountains on every coast is in direct proportion to the depth of the sea. If the sea is deep, the mountains are high, and there is always a corresponding increase or decrease between the mountains and the sea. This implies that they have been weighed and measured.

QUESTIONS

1. Instead of finding scientific error, what do we find the Bible to teach?
2. What truth is revealed by Genesis 1:9?
3. How would you show Ecclesiastes 1:7 to be scientifically correct?
4. What Scripture throws light upon Ecclesiastes 1:7?
5. Explain the scientific truth of Isaiah 40:12.

19

TEACHING THE TWO KINDS OF KNOWLEDGE

In our last lesson, we have been studying how to deal with the skeptical. We have taken up a number of seemingly scientific errors of the Bible.

However, this does not really solve the heart of the problem for the man who is skeptical toward the Bible as a whole. His difficulty lies in the fact that he is spiritually dead and dominated by the world mind.

Romans 8:7 tells us, *"The carnal* [world] *mind is enmity against God."*

The natural man receiveth not the things of the Spirit of God: for they are foolishness unto him: neither can he know them, because they are spiritually discerned. (1 Corinthians 2:14)

We need to show the skeptic that in the world, there are two kinds of knowledge. These two kinds of knowledge are the knowledge of the natural man and the knowledge that comes from revelation.

In showing a man the difference between the two, you must first show him the source, the limitations, and the insufficiencies of natural knowledge.

When we speak of the knowledge of natural man, we speak of the knowledge that the world has. It is the great accumulation of knowledge that fills our libraries and our textbooks; it is the embodiment of all that we know about reality.

Our first problem is: What is the source of this knowledge? The source is man's physical body and the material universe around him. We shall explain this more fully. Every contact that man has with the world comes to him through his five senses.

These five senses belong to the central nervous system—sight, hearing, touch, taste, and smell. Man knows nothing at all about reality except that which he has gained through these senses. You could picture for yourself how much a man would be able to know if he could not see, hear, touch, taste, or smell. The central nervous system gives us every contact that we have ever possessed with the rest of the world. Without it, we could know nothing at all about the world, the sky, the grass, the sea, or other human beings.

Helen Keller possessed only three senses: the sense of touch, the sense of taste, and the sense of smell. Her sense of touch was so developed that through it, under the direction of those who possessed the five senses, she gained a wide knowledge of the world and life.

However, if it were possible for a man to be born with none of the senses, he would never be able to be taught a thing. He could learn absolutely nothing of the outward world. He would have no avenue to his mind through which any knowledge could come to him. In this, we can see that the reasoning powers of the mind are dependent upon the material of sensation that is brought to it through the five senses.

To aid his senses in their search for reality, man has developed the microscope, the spectroscope, and the telescope. Yet these instruments have only aided his senses in their contact with the physical world. Through them, he has been able to study the universe and forms of life that otherwise would have been invisible to his sense of sight. Through the microscope, he has been able to study the minutest forms of life. He has come to a knowledge of bacteria and a knowledge of realms that he otherwise would never have been able to contact.

With the aid of the telescope, man has gained a vast knowledge of the heavenly universe. With his naked eye, man can only see from two to four thousand stars, but with the aid of the telescope, he can see hundreds of thousands. By using the spectroscope, he has been able to study the composition of the stars.

There are in the universe around us many physical forces that we cannot perceive with our physical senses. But man has developed instruments that are sensitive to these forces and will record them.

We could mention a great many other inventions that man has produced to aid his senses in his acquisition of the knowledge of the world, but we have not the space here.

Man has made great progress. He has become familiar with the laws, processes, and forces of nature. He has made them obey his command so that he could utilize them to his own gain. Out of years of research, study, and experimentation of not only the present, but also the past, man has built the great civilization that we have today.

Yet the source of this vast accumulation of knowledge is based upon man's sense perceptions of the physical universe. Every invention that he uses aids only his senses. These senses belong to the physical body. They contact matter and man's every contact, therefore, has been only with a material realm.

Study the above until it becomes real in your own mind, for in dealing with a man who has become materialistic and atheistic, you must first show him that the source of all the knowledge that he has, or any other man has, is really his physical body. His body, as it were, is the trap in which he is caught.

After you have shown this to the individual with whom you are working, show him the limitations of that knowledge. If you have made the above clear to him, it will not be hard to show him its limitations.

We can illustrate the limitations of our senses in giving to us a true picture of reality by the following: a blind man who had never possessed the sense of sight, and who had never come into contact with men who possess it, would think that he had a true picture of the world around him through his four senses. He would never be able to know that there existed a quality such as color, light, or darkness because he would have no sense that could perceive it or admit an understanding of that quality to his mind.

A man who had never possessed a sense of hearing and never come into contact with men who could hear would think that he knew the universe as it was through his four senses.

By this, we can readily see that it may be that man, with his five senses, does not contact every force of the universe in which he lives. We do know that his five senses limit him to the knowledge of matter only. Every invention that he could ever produce can only aid him in the knowledge of the physical.

In our next lesson, we will show you how it is that materialism and atheism have developed. When you understand this, you will be able to show a man the reason for his own atheism and materialism.

QUESTIONS

1. Why is it that the things of God are foolishness to the natural man?

2. What fact must you point out to the skeptic?

3. How would you explain the source of natural man's knowledge?

4. How would you explain to a skeptic the limitations of his knowledge?

20

EXPLAINING THE CAUSE OF MATERIALISM

In our last lesson, we said we would continue the study of the development of materialism and atheism. From what we have learned, we can now understand why it is that man has believed that there is nothing in the universe but matter and its properties.

He has said that man does not survive the existence of his physical body because there is no spiritual quality in man to exist after the body has disintegrated. We can see that such an attitude upon the part of man toward life is a natural attitude, for with his five senses to which he is limited, he can contact nothing but a physical world.

It would be just as logical for the blind man to refuse to believe that color existed as for man with his five senses to say that the spiritual does not exist.

A fish might just as well say that there is nothing outside of water as for man to say that in this universe, there exists nothing but matter.

We have seen that the source of man's knowledge is the central nervous system and its limitations are the physical universe and matter alone.

We do not want to give a wrong impression when speaking of the source of man's knowledge. Thinking does not arise out of sense perception. Man has capacities for thinking, reasoning, reflecting, and memorizing that are not based upon perception; yet man's mental powers and reasoning faculties have only the material of sensation from which to draw their conclusions.

Animals have sense perception; yet they do not have rational thinking. Rational thinking does not arise from sense perception. Yet our statement is true: man knows nothing except as it comes to his mind through one of his five senses.

In dealing with a man who professes to be a materialist and atheist, show him the above. Show him that the limitations of his knowledge are within the limits of matter and the utter fallacy of his refusing to believe that man is a spirit, or that God as a spiritual being exists.

Show him that one of two things must be true:

1. The scriptural teaching that man is a spirit being and the body is merely the home of the spirit.

2. The present-day attitude that man is only a physical being—that there is no spiritual quality in him, he is a part of nature just like a stick or stone, and he is only a physical mechanism.

Now, if the second attitude is true, there is no life after death and man need not prepare for death, or give it his attention here in this life. However, if the first teaching is true, we have no proof that man as a spiritual being does not survive the existence of his physical body. Explain to him that if this is true, it's a problem that he should not neglect. Since he has no proof that man is *not* a spirit being and can *never* prove it due to his five-sense limitations about the nature of reality, it is well worth his while to give the matter serious and sincere attention.

We cannot prove to a man that he is a spiritual being, nor can he prove to us that he is not a spiritual being. Merely because a doctor cannot locate the spirit in man by dissecting his dead body is not proof that man is not a spiritual being. The doctor only his sense of sight and physical instruments; as we have seen, the spiritual realm cannot be contacted by the physical.

The one with whom you are dealing and whom you have led this far might reply to you by stating that it could not be proven that man was a spirit and that he himself did not believe anything that he could not prove.

Your answer to him would be that it is a very hollow science that will not believe anything it cannot prove.

Show him that we have no knowledge within any sphere that is not based upon vast assumption. For example, in our knowledge of the outward world, we have to first assume that our senses do not deceive us. We could never prove that they give us a true picture of reality. We could never prove that our memory can be relied upon. We would only find ourselves arguing in circles if we attempted to prove these things.

However, we do believe that our senses tell us the truth because to do so works. We believe that grass is green, the pavement is hard, and all the other phenomena of nature.

Richard Acland Armstrong in writing about these facts has said: "These beliefs [referring to our belief in the external world, the veracity of memory, etc.] are justified in that they work. They never land us in confusion. They never break down. As the daily haps of life turn up, a myriad an hour in infinite diversity, the beliefs fit into them all without a jar or a contradiction. While, if for a moment we attempt to depart from them we fall into utter confusion. This is the highest evidence we can have."

In like manner, we assume that God exists, that we are spiritual beings capable of fellowship with Him, and that the Bible is a revelation from Him.

The only test that we can apply to these beliefs to prove whether they are true or not is the test that we applied to our knowledge of the outward world: does it work? Can we act upon the veracity of the Bible as we act upon our knowledge of the outward world? Does the Word never break down? Do we never land in confusion when we take what God says to be true?

When you have led a man this far, you can bring in something of your own personal experience. Show him that whenever you have acted upon the Bible, you have found that God comes upon the scene and that you therefore believe that you are justified in your belief.

Challenge him to make the same test. Tell him that if he is really sincere in wanting to know if God exists and He can fellowship, he can know the truth by acting upon God's Word. Give him Romans 10:9–10 and some of the other Scriptures that we have given you for leading a man to Christ. Tell him that if he will act upon them, God will make them good.

QUESTIONS

1. Explain why materialism has developed.

2. How would you show a man the utter fallacy of refusing to believe that man is a spirit?

3. How would you explain that all our knowledge is based upon assumption?

4. What facts would you present to cause a man to become concerned about his soul?

5. What challenge would you give a skeptic?

21

PRAYING WITH THE SICK

In this lesson, we will show you how to deal with a sick person for whom you are going to pray.

We are healed by acting upon the Word. The one who is sick must act upon the Word for his healing.

In my name…they shall lay hands on the sick, and they shall recover. (Mark 16:17–18)

If you pray for him according to this Scripture, he must act upon the Word that he shall recover.

In order to do this, he must be convinced in his mind of the fact that it is God's will to heal him. As long as a child of God has a doubt as to God's will in healing, he will not be able to positively act upon the Word, declaring that he is healed.

So the first thing is to show him from the Word that it is God's will to heal. In doing this, there are three things you must make clear:

1. Sickness and disease have their origins in spiritual death.

2. God's attitude toward disease.

3. How God has dealt with disease and the provision He has made for healing today.

THE ORIGIN OF DISEASE

Spiritual death, which entered the world by Adam's disobedience to God, has been the soil out of which has grown the reign of disease over man's body. If man had never died spiritually, his body would never have become subject to disease. Sin and disease are twins. They are both the works of Satan. Sin is a disease of the spirit; sickness is a disease of the body. They are not from God.

We can further see that sickness and disease originate in Satan by studying God's attitude toward disease.

GOD'S ATTITUDE TOWARD DISEASE

We can best find out what God's attitude is by studying the attitude of Christ, who came as the revealed will of God.

There are several instances where the attitude of Christ toward disease is clearly shown. One is found in Luke 13:10–17. On the Sabbath, after freeing a woman from an infirmity that she had had for eighteen years, Christ was criticized by the rulers of the synagogue.

His answer was, *"Ought not this woman...whom Satan hath bound, lo, these eighteen years, be loosed from this bond on the sabbath day?"* (verse 16). He plainly stated that Satan was the cause of the infirmity that had bound her physical body.

Another incident is found in Luke 5:18–25. A man with palsy is brought to the Lord and Christ said to him, *"Man, thy sins are forgiven thee"* (verse 20).

When the scribes and Pharisees questioned this statement, Christ replied, *"What reason ye in your hearts? Whether is easier,* to say, *Thy sins be forgiven thee; or to say, Rise up and walk?*" (verses 22–23).

In reality, Christ is saying, "Which is easier? What is the difference? To forgive sins that are the result of spiritual death, or to heal the disease of the physical body, which is also the result of spiritual death?" In either case, Christ was dealing with Satan's lordship over man.

Read Matthew 8:16–17 and Mark 1:32–34. This shows that it must have been God's will to heal, for Christ healed all who came to Him.

HOW GOD DEALT WITH DISEASE IN REDEMPTION

For this purpose the Son of God was manifested, that he might destroy the works of the devil.   (1 John 3:8)

Forasmuch then as the children are partakers of flesh and blood, he also himself likewise took part of the same; that through death he might destroy him that had the power of death, that is, the devil.   (Hebrews 2:14)

Since disease is Satan's work in man, if God is to destroy the works of Satan, He must deal with disease. He must provide a redemption for the body of man from disease as well as for the spirit from sin. God shows us in His Word clearly that He has made provision for the healing of man's body.

In Isaiah 53, the Holy Spirit has given to us a glimpse of what took place within the spirit of Christ when He was on the cross.

Surely our sicknesses he hath borne, And our pains—he hath carried them, And we—we have esteemed him plagued, Smitten of God, and afflicted. And he is pierced for our transgressions, Bruised for our iniquities, The chastisement of our peace [is] on him, And by his bruise there is healing to us. All of us like sheep have wandered, Each to his own way we have turned, And Jehovah hath caused to meet on him, The punishment of us all. (Isaiah 53:4–6 YLT)

God's Word reveals to us that when God made Jesus sin, He made Him to bear our disease and pain, which were also the products of spiritual death. At the same time that God laid upon Him our iniquity, He laid upon Him our diseases and pains, and because of His being bruised, by His bruising, we are healed from the power of disease.

Christ bore our sins and the penalty that we might be free from sin, its power, and its judgment. Upon the same ground, He bore our diseases and pain. He carried them that we might be set free, that we need not bear them. God made Him to be our sin-bearer and our sickness-bearer. Him who knew no sin was made sin and Him who knew no sickness was made sickness.

Christ's ministry upon the earth was twofold, constantly affecting the souls and bodies of men. His death was twofold, bearing our sins and diseases. He is the same today, and the twofold ministry of blessing for soul and body has continued from His earthly ministry to the present time.

He bore man's spiritual death that he might have life, and in His Word, He made provision for man's salvation. He bore man's diseases and in His Word, He made provision for man's healing.

In the commission He gave to His disciples to a world for whom He had died, He showed that the twofold ministry was to continue.

First, the commission is to meet the spiritual need of man: *"He that believeth and is baptized shall be saved"* (Mark 16:15). Then comes the second part of that commission, where He meets the need in man's body: *"In my name…they shall lay hands on the sick, and they shall recover"* (Mark 16:17–18).

Our right to the healing purchased for us in His redemption has been given to us in the authority of His name. This is what you must show to the individual before you pray for him. When he understands that healing is his to the extent that he will be able to act upon the Word of God, God will confirm His Word in his life as He confirmed it in the days of the apostles.

QUESTIONS

1. Why must a child of God know that it is God's will to heal him?

2. Explain the fact that disease did not come from God.

3. Give and explain several instances that reveal how Christ looked upon disease.

4. How has God dealt with disease?

5. What provision has God made for man's healing today?

22

HOW TO RECEIVE THE HOLY SPIRIT

You may come across people who have had erroneous teaching concerning the baptism of the Holy Spirit. You must first show them the scriptural meaning of the term.

It is first mentioned by John the Baptist:

I indeed baptize you with water unto repentance. But he that cometh after me is mightier than I, whose shoes I am not worthy to bear: he shall baptize you with the Holy Ghost, and with fire. (Matthew 3:11)

This statement is also recorded in Mark 1:8, Luke 3:16, and John 1:26–27.

After His resurrection, Christ refers to this promise made by John, commanding His apostles *"that they should not depart from Jerusalem, but wait for the promise of the Father, which, saith he, ye have heard of me. For John truly baptized with water; but ye shall be baptized with the Holy Ghost not many days hence"* (Acts 1:4–5).

Then the term "baptize" is also used by Peter in Acts 11:16 when he is speaking of the fact that the Holy Spirit came upon the gentiles in exactly the same manner that He did upon the Jews on the day of Pentecost.

The word "baptize" is an untranslated Greek word meaning to immerse.

Paul speaks of the baptism of the Holy Spirit in 1 Corinthians 12:13. Let us examine these Scriptures in order to learn the scriptural meaning of the term. When John the Baptist said, "He shall baptize you with the Holy Spirit," he was referring to eternal life that Christ made it possible for man to receive. John is comparing his ministry to that of Christ's. The baptism that he himself brings is physical. It does not touch the spirit, the real man. It is a type of the work that Jesus is to do within the spirit of man. John is saying, "I baptize the physical body with water, but He shall immerse the spirit with the Holy Spirit and out of that immersion shall come the new birth, and man shall begin a new life."

It was for this new birth that Christ was to bring that the disciples were told to tarry in Jerusalem. The Holy Spirit could not come to impart the life of God to man's spirit until Christ had been glorified, or until redemption had been complete. It is largely due to the fact that the church has not understood that the disciples were not born again until the day of Pentecost that has led to the erroneous teaching concerning the baptism of the Holy Spirit. Because it came on Pentecost, they have thought that it was a second experience, not realizing that no man could be born again before that day.

Let us now examine 1 Corinthians 12:13 to see whether it also refers to the new birth. *"For by one Spirit are we all baptized into one body."* When does a man become a member of the body of Christ? When he is born again. Again, we see that the term "baptize" refers to the new birth. The baptism into the body of Christ is the birth into that body.

> For as many of you as have been baptized into Christ have put
> on Christ.   (Galatians 3:27)

This refers to the new birth, for we are told in Romans 8:9, *"If any man have not the Spirit of Christ, he is none of his."*

Let us see what actually took place on the day of Pentecost. The disciples were gathered in the upper room in which they were sitting. They were filled with the Holy Spirit and they were immersed with the Holy Spirit.

The baptism in the Holy Spirit is reversed in a certain sense from baptism in water. In water baptism, there is a plunging down into the water. In the Spirit baptism, there is a coming down upon of the Holy Spirit. However, the result is the same: immersion. The disciples were immersed in the Holy Spirit, and out of that immersion, they were born again. Then came the second experience; they were filled with the Holy Spirit.

There is a vast difference between being baptized, immersed in the Holy Spirit, and being filled with the Holy Spirit. We may illustrate it by the following: if a tank were filled with water and a man was immersed in the water, he would be in the water but the water would not be in him.

The disciples could not be filled or indwelt by the Holy Spirit until they had been born again. Our conclusion is this: the phrase "baptism in the Holy Spirit" literally and scripturally refers to the new birth, and the second experience is to receive or be filled with the Holy Spirit. It is clear that the early church did not use the term "baptism" as reference to a second experience, the filling of the Spirit. After the day of Pentecost, it is used only once when Peter was relating what had happened when the gentiles first had received the gospel. He tells that the same thing that took place when they first believed upon Christ occurred again and he recalled the words of John the Baptist that Christ should baptize with the Holy Spirit.

HOW DOES ONE RECEIVE THE HOLY SPIRIT?

The Holy Spirit is received by faith. This is taught very definitely in Galatians:

This only would I learn of you, Received ye the Spirit by the works of the law, or by the hearing of faith? (Galatians 3:2)

That the blessing of Abraham might come on the Gentiles through Jesus Christ; that we might receive the promise of the Spirit through faith.   (Galatians 3:14)

What is faith? Faith is nothing more nor nothing less than acting upon the Word of God. Acting upon the Word of God is taking the Word of God as sufficient evidence above all other evidence. The Word declares that the heavenly Father will give the Holy Spirit to His children who ask Him. If we ask in faith that is acting upon His Word, we shall receive the Holy Spirit. We ask the Holy Spirit to come into our lives to fill us, then we act upon the Word that says that we shall receive Him when we ask, thanking Him for coming into our lives; and God must make that Word good. (See Luke 11:13.)

Nowhere are we taught that we should look upon tongues as the evidence of the fact that the Holy Spirit has filled us. The book of Acts is not doctrinal. It is historical. It relates that upon several occasions during a period of thirty-five years, certain ones spoke in tongues when they were filled with the Holy Spirit: Acts 2:4, the day of Pentecost; Acts 10:46, the day the gentiles received Christ; and in Acts 19:6, at Ephesus.

Speaking in tongues is only mentioned in several other places in Scripture. In 1 Corinthians 14, Paul writes to the Corinthians to reprove them for their abuse of tongues. First Corinthians 12:30 shows clearly that all do not speak in tongues, and 1 Corinthians 14:22 shows that tongues are not a sign for the believer, but for the unbeliever.

Not only does Scripture fail to teach that tongues is the evidence of the filling of the Holy Spirit, but to make tongues the evidence of the Holy Spirit's filling would be contrary to God's dealing with the new creation. The speaking in tongues is a physical manifestation and evidence to the senses of man. God has nowhere put a premium upon sense evidence, or ever permitted us to trust it. He is a faith God and everything we receive from Him we receive on the grounds of faith.

So in dealing with a person who desires to be filled with the Holy Spirit, show him that he shall receive the Holy Spirit when he acts upon Matthew 7:11 as he acted upon the Word for salvation.

A man is born again when he says, "I have eternal life because I have met the conditions of the Word and the Word declares it." A man is healed when he says, "I am healed because the Word declares, 'By His stripes, I am healed.'" Prayer is answered when we thank Him for the answer because the Word declares that what we ask, we shall receive. So also, the Holy Spirit comes into our lives when we say, "I have the Holy Spirit because the Father has promised to give the Holy Spirit to them who ask Him."

QUESTION

1. What is the difference between the baptism of the Spirit and the filling of the Spirit?

ABOUT THE AUTHOR

Dr. E. W. Kenyon (1867–1948) was born in Saratoga County, New York. At age nineteen, he preached his first sermon. He pastored several churches in New England and founded the Bethel Bible Institute in Spencer, Massachusetts. This school later became the Providence Bible Institute when it was relocated to Providence, Rhode Island.

Kenyon served as an evangelist for over twenty years. In 1931, he became a pioneer in Christian radio on the Pacific Coast with his show *Kenyon's Church of the Air,* for which he earned the moniker "The Faith Builder." He also began the New Covenant Baptist Church in Seattle.

In addition to his pastoral and radio ministries, Kenyon wrote extensively. Among his books are the Bible courses *The Bible in the Light of Our Redemption: From Genesis Through Revelation* and *Studies in the Deeper Life: A Scriptural Study of Great Christian Truths,* and more than twenty other works, including *The Wonderful Name of Jesus, Two Kinds of Faith, In His Presence: The Secret of Prayer, The Blood Covenant, The Hidden Man, Jesus the Healer, New Creation Realities,* and *Two Kinds of Righteousness.*